LATIN BY THE NATURAL METHOD

FIRST AND SECOND YEAR

TEACHER'S MANUAL

By
William G. Most Ph. D.

MEDIATRIX PRESS

MMXV

ISBN: 0692566864

Latin by the Natural Method Teacher's Guide
©Mediatrix Press 2015
This edition may not be reproduced for commercial purposes, nor electronically as a whole without permission of the publisher.

This work is in the public domain.
Reprinted from the 1962 Revised Edition.

Mediatrix Press
607 E. 6th Ave. Ste. 230
Post Falls, ID 83854
www.mediatrixpress.com

Table of Contents

I. History of Latin Methods. 1

II. General Principles of the Natural Method. 11

III. Specific Suggestions for Presenting Each Lesson. . . 39

Comments on Individual Lessons. 40

Suggestions for Teaching Second Year 86

Specific Suggestions.. 88

Key to Year I. English to Latin 93

Key to Year II. Scrambles
And English to Latin.. 125

How Do You Say it Department. 139

I. HISTORY OF LATIN METHODS

Present deficiencies: Most Latin teachers will readily admit that Latin is not taught with very great success today. Even after as much as eight years of Latin, students often find it quite an effort to translate fifty lines of Cicero in an hour and even then, they will not always get the sense.

Things were not always thus: for about a thousand years after Latin ceased to be a native language, it was taught with far greater success, so that students, even those of very ordinary intelligence, actually learned to read, write, and speak the language fluently. The methods used then were not very much like the method that has now come to be considered as "traditional." Actually, the so-called traditional methods today go back only to about the 16th century. History shows a constant decline in the popularity of Latin and in the ability of students ever since that "traditional" method was introduced. To cite but a few figures: in 1910, 49.05% of the students in American High Schools took Latin. By 1934 that figure had dropped to 16.04% and by 1954, to 7%. Of this small group it is estimated that about 95% drop the language after two years. (Part of the drop is probably due to the fact that formerly a much smaller percentage of students attended high school. These had less choice of subjects, and, often, more eagerness to learn, precisely because the opportunity was less common).

Latin by the Natural Method

<u>Former more successful methods:</u> During the Middle Ages, students began the study of Latin between the ages of 5 and 7. The method used was the purely direct method (we do not propose here to revive a purely direct method, for reasons to be indicated later. Rather, we would use its basic principles and advantages and combine them with additional techniques suited to the difference in the age at which students today begin Latin). Only very easy materials were used for reading, chiefly dialogues. Works like Caesar, and Cicero's orations, even when they came to be used commonly, were not attempted until after the student had spent from 3 to 5 years on easier materials. The result was that when he finally did begin to study these works, he was in a good position to gain a real appreciation of them, for he had learned by that time to read, write, and speak Latin with fluency.

<u>The rejection of Medieval Latin:</u> When in 1444, Lorenzo Valle published his *Elegantiae Latini Sermonis*, he called Medieval Latin barbarous, and called for imitation of ancient models. His goal was worthy; yet, as Sandys says (*Companion to Latin Studies*, Cambridge, 1938, p. 850) in effect, he was really "dealing a death-blow to the natural and colloquial use of the living language, and unconsciously promoting the growth of a servile Ciceronianism". For if his suggestion had been taken moderately, it would have been quite beneficial, but extremists came to think that ONLY Ciceronian Latin was good: for them, every phrase and word which could not be found in Cicero had to be rejected.

<u>A living Language changes:</u> The truth that some failed to see is that a living language has to change and to grow. In so doing, it may become better or worse as a language, but

the mere fact that it changes does not mean it declines. If it did, we should have to condemn Chaucer for changing the language of Beowulf, and we would also condemn Shakespeare for departing from Chaucerian rules—not to mention what judgment would be passed upon modern. English, which has departed still farther. These extremists seemed to think that to change Ciceronian rules was to decay. Thus they would speak of Cicero as the center of a Golden Age—after him, came Silver Latin—and finally—shades of Nabuchodonosor's statue!—would come the age of Iron and Clay—which is what the lexicographer Forcellini called the age of St Augustine! We wonder what Forcellini would have said about the Italian of Dante, a further stage in the alleged decay of Latin!

<u>When is a language a good language?</u> Let us approach the problem carefully: How shall we judge the merit of these periods, or the works written in them? There are two very different questions to be asked, and the answers may differ.

<u>Is it a good means of communication?</u> First of all, we ought to ask: Is the language of a given period better or worse as a means of communication? The chief purpose of a language is to convey thought. It ought to do this with ease, accuracy, beauty, and so on. In the measure in which it does this, it is a good means of communication; in the measure in which it fails, it is poor as a language. If we compare Late Latin, the language of St. Augustine, with the Latin of Cicero, what do we find? We find that Late Latin is not "just as good" as Ciceronian: it is actually superior! For if a language as such ought to convey thought with ease and accuracy, who could fail to see that the language of St. Augustine, with its more abundant and freer constructions,

its much richer vocabulary and clarity gained by increased use of prepositions, provides a means of conveying thought that is much easier to use, and more accurate at the same time?

The vocabulary of Ciceronian Latin is very noticeably smaller than that of Late Latin. This is particularly true of abstract nouns. The result is that Cicero often finds it necessary to devise a phrase or relative clause, where Late Latin (or Greek, or modern English) would express the idea with one word. Not infrequently, the one word would be clearer than the circumlocution.

Furthermore, the constructions used in Late Latin were often much more logical. For example, Early Latin (the period before Cicero) used the indicative in indirect questions (as Greek also does). There is no logical or historical reason why such a clause, which deals with a question of fact should have to have subjunctive (the subjunctive, historically, deals with ideas of will). Cicero's age made the subjunctive the rule, quite illogically. Late Latin returned to a notable extent to the more logical indicative of Early Latin, and Greek. Again, Late Latin uses freely the dico quod indirect statement, a perfectly logical structure, in contrast to the objective-infinitive, in which, contrary to all logic, the objective is made to be the case of the subject. The quod type was in use in everyday conversational Latin (and a parallel structure in Classical Greek) long before the age of Late Latin. It appeared occasionally in literature at a very early date, e.g., Plautus (Asin. 52) wrote this line: "*scio iam, filius quod amet meus istanc meretricem*", using the quod structure. The reason why Plautus did so is very interesting: in this example (as in so many other instances) the objective-infinitive structure would be ambiguous, while the <u>quod</u> structure is entirely clear!

Cicero's age made wide use of cases alone, without prepositions. The genitive and dative are not particularly difficult to follow. Some ablatives without prepositions are easy enough to understand. But some ablatives are quite vague, lacking in precision. In general, the English prepositions that could be supplied to translate an ablative without a preposition are: "in, by, with, from, because, of, in accordance with." Of course, the context makes clear (sometimes only after reflection) which is the correct meaning. But would we not have a clearer and more accurate means of communication if we added prepositions to show precisely which sense is meant? Late Latin uses far more prepositions than Ciceronian Latin, and thereby gains an unmistakable advantage.

The fact is, that Cicero and most of the "Classical" authors were using a somewhat affected form of the language, quite different from that employed in everyday speech. Hence, G. Showerman spoke of Classical Latin as "never the facile language of the people" and added that during the Late period the older literary Latin was "a resisting medium that was foreign to the general run of men" (*Horace and His Influence*, Boston, 1922, p. 90). And the ancient rhetorician Quintilian warns his budding orators not to employ the artificially compressed style of Sallust ("Sallustiana brevitas") when trying to persuade a court (<u>Institutiones Oratoriae</u> X.1.32).

We conclude, therefore, that <u>as an instrument of communication</u>, the language of the Late period is not only equal, but superior to that of Cicero.

Latin by the Natural Method

<u>Are works of artistic beauty written in it?</u> The second question to be asked is this: What is the artistic merit of works produced in the various periods of the history of Latin? Here we freely concede that in both the "Classical" and in the Late period, we find quite a variety: both periods produced works that are excellent artistically—and both periods produced works of little or no artistic merit. In judging the merit of these works, one must take care to avoid the worship of "Sacred Cows": not everything ancient, not everything by a Father of the Church is fine literature. But, if we compare individual works with individual works, we must say that there are creations of towering beauty from both pagan and patristic pens. To mention but a few: the <u>Aeneid</u> of Vergil and the <u>Odes</u> of Horace certainly deserve a place among the masterpieces of all ages—but so do the Confessions and City of God of St. Augustine, and many of the works of St. Cyprian.

There is, however, one consideration that is often overlooked in this matter: true art aims at producing beauty. And all beauty is but a reflection of some bit of the infinite Beauty of God. Now is it at all likely that a man such as Vergil, whose highest "ideal" is the adulterous and lying Jupiter, is it likely that a man who knows nothing greater than such a "god" could reflect the real beauty of God as well as a Saint Augustine whose great soul had contemplated the transcendent splendor of true Divinity? It is not strange that lists of the world's greatest literature invariably praise his <u>Confessions</u> —and are equally apt to pass by in silence, the wars of Caesar, which are well written indeed, but reveal no more literary genius than do the memoirs of Churchill, which are equally well written.

Teacher's Manual

<u>The beginning of the grammar-analysis method:</u> But let us return to those who went to extremes in their imitation of Cicero. They, not understanding these facts, ridiculed Medieval Latin, preferring instead an extreme imitation of Cicero. Their numbers increased. There were a few who protested, such as Erasmus, who, in 1528, satirized the pedantic style of Bembo, Latin secretary to Pope Leo X. But soon Erasmus found himself attacked, by a man bearing the very anachronistic (and un-Christian) name of Julius Caesar Scaliger, who in 1531 published an oration claiming that Cicero was absolutely perfect.

Schoolmasters finally went over to the position defended by Scaliger, with the result that the grammar-analysis method, the "traditional" method of teaching Latin was introduced, with its minute imitation of Cicero, having as its chief objective, to translate and parse a certain number of lines of Latin per day. It is not strange that the effectiveness of Latin teaching declined, and that the language, being forbidden to use any non-Ciceronian words, was unable to express the new concept and to describe the new things that appeared as civilization matched on.

Formerly Latin had been a necessary tool for any man who aspired to advance himself, not only in the Church, but in any secular field whatsoever, for the lectures in the Universities, the debates in the parliaments, and the learned books even on natural science, were all written in Latin. But now that Latin had been made difficult by a too rigid adherence to Ciceronian details, and was no longer allowed to develop and keep pace with new developments, practical men turned to the vernaculars.

Latin by the Natural Method

<u>Change in objectives of Latin teaching</u>: Latin teachers, finding one of the chief motives for studying Latin removed, had to find new objectives to uphold. It was about this time that John Locke proposed the theory that schools were primarily for mental discipline, rather than for conveying a content of knowledge to the pupils. The vague implication was that somehow the pupil would acquire the knowledge after graduation: his schooling would be merely an exercise, a mental discipline. (For a very fine study of the historical matter, cf. George E. Ganss S.J. <u>St. Ignatius' Idea of a Jesuit University</u>, Marquette U. Press, 2nd ed.1956, pp. 218-58).

<u>The Classical Investigation and mental discipline</u>: Mental discipline is still the goal of most textbooks used in today's teaching of Latin. In 1924, the Classical Investigation proposed 19 objectives, but did not include the ability to speak Latin, and rated the ability to read Latin at sight in the lowest place. The result was that the real goals aimed at by the "traditional" method are now two: 1. mental discipline, 2. cultural values.

The noted grammarian C. Bennett loudly acclaims mental discipline. Speaking of the ability to read Latin without translating (the way in which a native would read it, the only way in which it can be read with ease), Bennett said: "Those, now, who insist so strenuously on the importance of the direct subjective interpretation of Latin [the ability to read freely without translating] at the very outset of the study seem to me to advocate the acquisition of something which . . . if attained, is not likely to be of any greater educational utility then the capacity to understand colloquial French or German which an American lad might acquire by a moderate period of foreign residence. . . .

Teacher's Manual

Would not the chief usefulness of Latin AS AN INSTRUMENT OF INTELLECTUAL DISCIPLINE vanish the moment the mind of the pupil passed from its objective to its subjective contemplation? So soon as such a transition was effected, all need of translation would at once disappear, and with it THOSE MINUTE AND SEARCHING MENTAL PROCESSES WHICH CONSTITUTE THE MOST IMPORTANT FUNCTIONS OF THE STUDY. AND WHICH GIVE 'IT ITS SUPERIOR TITLE TO A PLACE IN THE CURRICULUM. . . ." (Emphasis added. Cited from D. White, The Teaching of Latin, Chicago, 1941,pp. 132-33) and, a bit further on Bennett adds: ". . . after thirty years of continuous study of Latin I am still bound to confess that I think it hard, very hard."

Latin for cultural values: As for attaining cultural values, we need to face the issue realistically. Even in English, where there is no language barrier, it is difficult to convey true literary appreciation to young students. In Latin, the difficulty is increased, whatever the method of teaching used. The difficulty is especially great, however, if we make mental discipline the chief goal of Latin teaching, at the expense of what Bennett calls the "direct subjective interpretation", that is, the ability to read freely without translating.

Conclusion: The goal chosen will determine the means to be taken. If one wishes to make Latin primarily a means of mental discipline, then he should choose the "traditional" method. If, however, one makes it his goal to teach students to read, write, and speak the language with fluency, then he will need to return to the basic principles of the method by which for literally a thousand years students were given

Latin by the Natural Method

that ability. The words of Professor Bossing relative to the teaching of modern languages apply equally well to the teaching of Latin:

"For example modern languages in high school and university are at once the poorest and possibly the best taught subjects in the curriculum, depending upon the purpose one attributes to the teaching. If knowledge of grammatical form or an etymological study of language has been the prime purpose of linguistic study, then it would seem necessary to concede that modern-language teaching has been exceedingly well done. If, on the other hand, the main objective of modern language teaching has been to give to the student easy facility in reading or speaking the language, then the conclusion is unavoidable that no subject in the curriculum has been more atrociously taught or studied. This has been because teachers have not forced themselves and their students to square their methods critically with a clear-cut purpose. Language teaching with primary emphasis upon grammar can result only in mastery of the niceties of grammatical forms. Ease in reading and speaking are psychologically inhibited by the method. Not inapplicable is the homely story of the centipede who managed his many legs very efficiently until asked how he performed such a feat; whereupon he landed paralyzed in a ditch beside the road, unable, consciously, to get his legs to act in easy coordination. There is only one royal road to a speaking use of a language and that is to speak it, just as the only sure route to an easy reading knowledge of a language is to read it. Attention to grammar should be incidental, if not omitted entirely, until facility in speaking or reading the language has been acquired."

Bossing, Nelson, Teaching in Secondary Schools (3rd ed. Boston: 1952) pp. 201-202.

Teacher's Manual

II. GENERAL PRINCIPLES OF THE NATURAL METHOD

WE shall not, however, merely take over the medieval procedure bodily: for the age at which students begin Latin today is much different from that at which students formerly began. That age difference calls for some adjustment. Therefore it seems best that we employ a semi-direct method, one that will endeavor to incorporate the basic advantages of the direct method, and to add to it certain shortcuts based on the fact that students of High School age are capable of and inclined to make use of their reasoning faculty.

Key principle: automatic habits: From the older methods we borrow our basic principle: LEARNING A LANGUAGE IS REALLY LEARNING A SET OF HABITS. Therefore, our principal and basic technique will be to develop habits. To develop a set of linguistic habits, it is necessary to have frequent, extensive contact with large quantities of matter that is never too difficult, relative to a given stage of the student's development. Here, in passing, we may note a major failure of the "traditional" method: once the student has been given a drilling in the fundamentals of grammar (at the end of the 1st or the middle of second year), he is not given some material to read that will be moderately easy relative to his stage of development: rather, he is thrust into Caesar's wars, whose difficulty is such that throughout even eight years of Latin he will never see anything greatly more difficult. In other words, the "traditional" method does

Latin by the Natural Method

little to observe the principle that matter for beginners should be graded in difficulty. It is as though a piano teacher were to assign nothing but Chopin and Liszt to students who had been just taught the rudiments of the instrument. We shall, therefore, employ the rules not of Ciceronian, but of Late Latin; which is the better, the more normal, and less affected form of the language, and which is much better adapted to beginners. Only later, when a student has acquired facility in the easier forms of Latin, will he be given the usual readings from pagan authors. By that time he will have a better hope of readily appreciating them.

<u>The sense is paramount:</u> Furthermore, the material given should be so presented that *the chief emphasis will be on getting the sense.* Grammatical identifications and labels are used only when really necessary. For this purpose, we must part company with the "traditional" way of giving numbered, isolated sentences, taken from contexts of Cicero or Caesar which the student has not yet seen. Instead we shall use continuous narratives, and, where exercises are needed, they will be at least partially continuous, and all built upon the context of stories that have been seen previously. Thus from the start we train students to pay chief attention to the sense, and to use the help that one normally gets in reading or listening, from the fact that he is following the thought.

How the student should prepare a passage: The student's study habits will need to be changed sharply, in order to carry out this habit forming technique. He should be instructed to prepare a reading passage as follows:

Teacher's Manual

1. Let him read through a sentence or a group of sentences, trying to follow as much of the thought as he can without translating, and without thinking of English. When he attempts this on the first few days, of course he will not do it perfectly. But if he follows instructions it will only be a few days before he is able to do much of it. One of the chief problems is to convince him that such a thing is possible, that it can be done by very ordinary people, and is not reserved for the unusually bright. We must drill into him, repeating it many times in the year, that little Roman children before the use of reason could do this, that little natives of any country can do it, that even morons in every country can do it.

2. If he has not understood fully, on this first reading, then let him translate. (The first year book has all vocabulary on the margin. But later when he reads other books that do not have marginal vocabulary, he must be warned not to begin by looking up word.: so often a Latin word has many meanings—<u>which one is right can be determined only after one has the general thought of the sentence</u>. Therefore it is dangerous to look up words too early—try to guess, and get as much as possible of the sense first). IF HE SIMPLY MUST (this is reserved for emergency use only) let him look for and find: SUBJECT, VERB, OBJECT, in each clause, and translate them IN THAT ORDER. If this procedure is followed, seldom will a student need to be stalled on a difficult sentence. But it is emergency procedure only—to use it regularly would be to change to the "traditional" grammar-analysis approach.

3. But now the student has, by translating found the sense. Let him be sure it fits with the sense of previous sentences.

Latin by the Natural Method

<u>But if he stops at this point, he has lost a great advantage:</u> for he should next REREAD THE ENTIRE SENTENCE OR PASSAGE AT LEAST SIX TIMES, trying constantly to follow without thinking of any English words. At first, of course, he will find some trouble excluding English words completely. Let him not worry about that, but persevere. After a while he will learn to follow without thinking of English. Further, he will also learn to understand new, previously unseen passages without translating. The reason for this rereading is plain: it is to form habits. In this way the student becomes familiar with many patterns of structure, as well as vocabulary, endings etc. It is the most efficient and natural way to learn all these things. When he has reread many passages in this way, the student builds up a set of habits that operate automatically, without effort on his part. Only thus can he ever learn to handle the language with real freedom. It is difficult to persuade some students to do this rereading. <u>Actual experience shows, however, that even without rereading, students can do reasonably well, though not of course, nearly so well as if they had done it.</u>

It is very helpful, if he will not disturb others, to have me student read the passages aloud when studying.

<u>Teaching conversational Latin:</u> it is extremely valuable (though not strictly essential to the method) to use spoken Latin in class. Experience shows that even a teacher who is not accustomed to it can, by following the directions given here, grow in it along with the class. Spoken Latin greatly increases class interest.

The first step is for the teacher to ask questions in Latin about the story at the start of each lesson (see samples on

Teacher's Manual

pp. 27-28). The questions will need to be carefully prepared but it is not necessary to write them out, and especially, it would not be good to bring a written copy to class for it would cause the class to lose confidence. At first the teacher should ask questions which can be answered merely by repeating the teacher's sentence with one word changed, e.g., "*Quis habuit parvum agnum?*" "*Maria habuit parvum agnum.*" Of course, the text does not supply the words *Quis, Quid* etc. in the first few lessons. But the class will easily pick up the few special words needed if the teacher puts them on the board.

The next stage will require the students to give answers out of the book. Ask a series of questions on the opening story of each lesson, taking the story in normal sequence (at least for some time) such that the answer can be given by reading a phrase or sentence from the book. If the student does this, it will be clear that he has understood the oral question (and no problem of ponies here!) and also that he has understood the story, since he could find the answer in it. It is true, at first he may do some guessing, by finding in the text words similar to those in the question: but as time goes on, the teacher can so word the questions as to make that method impossible in many sentences.

To advance to the third stage, the teacher will, as the year goes on, begin to summarize (see a sample, p. 20 below) in his own words in Latin, some of the previous part of the story leading up to the current part of the story. This need not be done every day— every few lessons will suffice. At first he will merely watch eyes to see if there are signs of understanding, and will not ask questions during the summary, but only in the current part of the story. But after a few such summaries, he can occasionally inject questions into the summary, and then, of course, the answer will have

Latin by the Natural Method

to come in the student's own words, without help of the book.

A further device can be used when the first and second person forms are taken, by telling the class: "Any student called on today will be (e.g.) Abraham. He must answer questions about his life in the first person, and I will speak in the second person."

Some students take quickly to this spoken Latin— others will need some prodding. A few probably will not do it at all. It is best for the most part not to call on students by name for answers: fear might block their answers. It is better to accept volunteers, though at times one can call on some of the sluggish ones. But as long as a student can handle the other parts of the work well, he can be given a passing mark, for the conversation should not be strictly required.

It will be found helpful to provide a "psychological crutch" for the students, particularly

when speaking about something not covered in a page that is open at the time. That is, it helps give the students a sense of security to have the teacher point frequently at a map, while describing historical movements, or, if one wishes to talk at times on other subjects, to point at various objects. Thus, for example, one could produce a Rosary, and while holding it and pointing at various parts of it, he can name the parts, make simple statements about the contents of each mystery etc. One can also draw on the board the floor plan of a church, putting in the altar, and its fittings, the stations, etc., and describing each item simply.

Oral question tapes are available for both first and second year (sets MQ 13 and MQ 23). The tape first gives a Latin summary of the story (early in first year it uses the actual text from the book), then oral questions on the story.

Teacher's Manual

After each question there is a pause for the student to answer, then the tape gives one form of the answer in Latin.

Oral Latin examinations can be easily made as follows (optional): First tell a purely fictional, easy story in Latin. (Pick a story the class is unlikely to have read elsewhere). Ask the class to take notes on the content (do not collect the notes). After the story is complete, give a set of objective questions in Latin on the content of the story. Questions can be given in writing or orally: if orally, repeat each question twice. Allow students to ask questions in Latin, if questions seem unclear to them: answer them in Latin. This type of exam should not supplant the special exams suggested below, p.26.

Latin Word Order: It is the subject, verb and object that carry the greater part of the meaning of each clause. The mind, then, must readily pick these out. In English we do it by means of word order. In Latin it is done by means of endings. That means that Latin word order can be much freer than English. The pattern practices provided for lessons 1 and 2 (in the tape script, which may be used orally in class or in the lab on tapes) begin to accustom the student to this difference. In lesson 20 further practice is to be given. Explain again to the students that little Marcus did not have to rearrange his Mother's words into English word order—obviously that was impossible. He could follow them as they came. Here is a sample of how it felt to him (we are making it much more express and explicit then it was to him, of course: for him it was an automatic habit, more feeling than intellectual process). Suppose he heard: Maria agnum habuit. He would feel: "Maria"—Mary is doing something or involved in something. "Agnum"—She is doing something to the lamb. "Habuit"—She had the lamb.

Latin by the Natural Method

Let the students give such comments on following sentences (some are modified a bit) from <u>Exerceamus</u> of lessons 20-24. 20: Romani Carthaginem viderunt, Romani arma videre voluerunt (read last 2 words as unit). Masinissa, rex Numidiae, Carthaginem lacessivit. Romani etiam Corinthum deleverunt. (After they have commented on each sentence, reread the sentence a few times, asking then to follow sense without translating). 21: Marcus Caesarem videre voluit. Gracchus novam legem proposuit. Senatores hanc legem non amaverunt. Plebs novam legem amavit. 22. Marcus scholam aedificat. Roma multas consuetudines habet. Nemo agnum ex schola. expellit. Servus pecuniam non habet. 23. Romani Iugurtham punire volunt. Romani bellum movent. Marius exercitum meliorem facere sperat. Ille agros et pecuniam multam promisit. 24: Romani aurum amant. Mithradates veritatem dicit. Ergo Mithradates aurum in guttur dat, Auro accepto, ille caput calidum habuit. (It would be good also if the teacher gives such comments on the whole of the Exerceamus of 20.)

In lesson 25, we introduce sentences with two clauses: a main line and a sidetrack. We recognize a side track by the switch—words like, <u>quia</u>, <u>quod</u>, <u>quando</u> etc. Use the Scramble of lesson 25, with the following 4 step procedure: 1. Teacher gives whole sentence with comments, e.g., <u>Sulla</u>—Sulla doing something or involved in something. <u>In urbem</u>—into the city. <u>Quia</u>—because (opens the sidetrack; we will not get back to the main line until the side track is complete). <u>Marium</u>—someone, probably Sulla, is doing something to Marius. <u>Timuit</u>—he feared Marius: (thought seems complete, sidetrack may be complete), in spoken form, oral phrasing, while in printed form, commas usually help show the end of side tracks; we should get back to main line now. <u>Rursus</u>— again. <u>Venit</u>—Sulla came back into the city. 2. And now the whole sentence: *Sulla in urbem, quia Marium timuit, rursus venit*—which means: Sulla came back into the city, because he feared Marius. 3. And now you try it (Now repeat it in same phrasing, having students give comments). 4. Repeat whole sentence in Latin 5 times, asking them to follow without translating. Then do the same with the entire Scramble in lessons 25-28 inclusive.

In lesson 39 we notice that now that we have objective-inf., the objective will not always mean that someone is doing something to the person in the objective; for the person in the objective may be the subject of an infinitive, and so may be doing something. So if we meet an objective how can we tell? Easily. We learned that Caesar in the nominative could mean either "C is doing something" or "C is involved in something." The "involved" took care of possibility that someone might be doing something to <u>Caesar</u>, e.g., C interfectus est a Bruto. Similarly, an objective, e.g., <u>Marcum</u> can mean that someone is doing something to M, or that M is doing something or involved in something. How to tell the difference? Simply by the <u>combination of words</u> used and by the <u>whole thought</u>. After all, that is the way we have been handling nominative up to now, even if we did not realize it. So let us practice. Give the sentence: Paulus dixit Marcum venire. How do we know what to do with Marcum? Easily. First, the dixit shows us that an indirect statement is probably coming. Then, right after <u>Marcum</u> we find <u>venisse</u>, which settles it for sure. But suppose the word order had been different: Marcum venire dixit Paulus. Here is how it would feel: <u>Marcum</u>—Someone may be doing something to M, or he is involved in something or doing something. <u>To make it simple, let us agree to say merely: "M is involved in something."</u> That lets us suspend judgment until we hear a few more words.

<u>Venisse</u>—seems that M is coming. <u>Dixit</u>—someone said he was coming. <u>Paulus</u>—Paul said it. (Now repeat sentence 4 times.) Now have the students practice on following: *Fabium vivere dixit Paulus. Clodium esse malum dixit Cicero.* Then use ind. statement sentences of Scrambles of lessons 39-41 same way. Call for the same type of word order practice on Scrambles in lessons 51 & 52.

Note that special minor word order pattern is taught in lesson 30. Other special patterns will be taught in second year.

If the student works diligently on this sort of practice, he can learn to follow even the most interwoven sentences without translating.

Beginning in lesson 25, we have three types of word order: easy, medium, hard. There is a certain value to be had from each kind. At the beginning of the course, the student is probably rather afraid of the subject. So we try to introduce new features slowly: hence word order almost like English is used for some time, especially in the first 19 lessons. Such word order actually does occur in Latin, though infrequently in the oldest matter. But it permits the student to conquer some of his fear and to get an easy start. As time goes on, we systematically wean him away from the easier word orders.

The above word order practice is available in the repetitive tapes (set MR 130 for first year. Similar matter for second year is part of set MRP 283). These tapes also give parts of the *Exerceamus* and the complete Scrambles three times: 1. Continuous reading and moderate speed is to be followed without translating. 2. Reading in phrases, with pauses for repetition: phrasing is of varied types, to accustom students the better to follow without translation

Teacher's Manual

3. Continuous reading at high speed (speed increases as year advances) to be followed without translating.

    Pattern practice: The 1st year tape script and the second year book give abundant pattern practice. In it, students are asked to manipulate sentences or clauses, sometimes by filling in, sometimes by paraphrasing, sometimes by making other changes. First an example is given and worked out for the student. Then he does the same with many other examples, each on the same pattern. This work can be done either orally in class or with tapes. If done without tapes, for some exercises the class can answer in unison, for others it is better to have student answer one after the other rapidly, according to seating position in class. This practice is designed to develop automatic habits, and is very useful. However, it would be <u>a great mistake to fail to see its limitations</u>. For, precisely because it comes in a preset situation, with many similar examples, a student can fall into merely mechanical responses, without understanding the thought. Earnest students can easily avoid this. But even the earnest student will need much normal in-context matter as a supplement. For the transfer from pattern practice to normal context uses of the same patterns is far from 100%. If a teacher listens to a class running down these patterns, he may easily get the illusion that they are doing wonderfully well—and then on trying to get them to do the same patterns in context, he will find that they have profited, but that the transfer is far below 100%. However, the texts provide both elements, both patterns and abundant natural large context matter: thus the advantages of both types of work are gained. Tapes are available (set MP 183 for first year: set MRP 283 for second year contains both patterns and repetitive matter).

Latin by the Natural Method

<u>The use of tapes</u>: As many years of experience have shown, this method can and does operate very successfully without any tapes whatsoever. Yet tapes do provide a valuable help. It is obvious that tapes can be a great help in developing automatic habits. They provide a concentrated form of study: while in the normal classroom, a student answers once or twice in a period, with the tape machine in a lab, he must answer dozens of times in the same period. They also help deal with the problem of shyness: students who freeze in class often feel secure in the lab booth. Some psychologists think that tapes, by giving auditory and speaking practice, cultivate a sort of motor muscle memory. Of course, oral practice without tapes gives some of the same. If every class is held in the lab, a class can be divided (after the teacher gets to know them) into perhaps three segments. While 2 segments are working on tapes, the teacher gives explanations "live" and answers questions for another segment. Thus each segment can be allowed to advance at its own natural speed, independently of the others. The teacher can arrange to listen to recitations via the switchboard part of the time: in the regular classroom, he heard only one or two answers per period of each student anyway. However, provision must be made for considerable precise translation of large in-context passages even if all periods are held in the lab. This could be done "live" or by making translation tapes (part of sentence—pause—translation). If lab is used only for one or two periods per week, then tapes corresponding to lessons covered in the previous classes can be used for that period. Moreover, on any basis, it is of great importance to get students to spend as much time as possible in private tape practice. This should not, however, supplant all of the more usual type of class preparation; especially one needs to

Teacher's Manual

beware of the illusion mentioned above that can come from pattern work.

<u>Active and passive mastery of language:</u> A secondary, but <u>extremely important</u> feature of this method is based on the distinction between active and passive mastery on the part of the students. A student has passive mastery of a form or structure if he can understand and translate it when he sees it or hears it. He has, in addition, active mastery, if he can make such a form or structure for himself. It is natural that passive mastery should develop much more rapidly than active mastery. Therefore, the teacher should <u>take care not to insist on complete active mastery of each new item shortly after it is introduced</u>: It is sufficient to attain mostly passive mastery in the first year, with, of course, some active ability. But more active mastery can be demanded in second year (see the suggestions for teaching second year). <u>If too much active mastery is demanded not only will the method suffer in general, but it will be impossible to complete the first year book in a year.</u>

<u>Presenting verb forms:</u> This distinction has special consequences in the matter of learning verb forms. A study by W. Strain (*Classical Journal*, Vol. 33, pp. 18-24) shows that about 91% of all verbs forms met in the usual (traditional) second year texts are in the third person. It is obvious that this is true of most Latin authors that a student will read. The consequence is obvious: in first year it is better to demand active mastery only of third person forms, being content with mostly passive control of the 1st and 2nd person forms. And, of course, less emphasis should be placed on the passive forms of the verb than on the active. In practice, this means that in form tests, one will do well to

Latin by the Natural Method

use almost exclusively third person forms when calling for English to Latin forms, reserving the other forms for the Latin to English section, where recognition is sufficient. And the percentage of passive forms called for should be much lower than that of active forms. For this reason this text presents 3rd person forms first, waiting until about the middle of the year before introducing 1st and 2nd person forms.

This text also begins with the perfect tense. The beginner in Latin probably has never heard of such things as declension and conjugation. We must present one of these concepts at the outset, but it is a great help if we can hold off on the other, until the first has been assimilated. Since all conjugations are the same in the perfect, we can refrain from mention of the concept of conjugation for some time, while we are presenting declensions. The use of the perfect also makes it possible to write less unnatural stories, since most narratives are usually written in the perfect, not in the present.

In presenting a new set of forms, it is best to try to establish a direct relation between the English and the Latin expressions, so that the grammatical description, though it will be mentioned, does not come in between the English and the Latin meanings. That is, we do not say: Now how do we form the future indicative active third singular of love? Instead we say: "He will love" etc. If a student must first identify a form as future indicative active third singular etc. and only then obtain the equivalent, there is an unnecessary middle step injected into the work of translating. Such a step is needless, and makes it difficult to learn to understand without translating, which is an important goal. It is still better if the student learns to

Teacher's Manual

understand new forms without translating: this is quite possible if he will do the rereading described.

<u>Presenting declensions</u>: When a student faces a sentence for the first time, his mind must automatically pick out the subject, verb, and object. In English, this is done by means of word order; in Latin it is done by endings. This difference needs to be grasped by the student, but not necessarily in the first few lessons: it is well to mention it <u>lightly</u>, at the start, and to stress it more about lesson 20, when more difficult word orders begin. But, in order that the student may acquire <u>automatic habits</u> of picking out subject, verb and object easily, he should have suitable mental and habitual groups of endings. Thus, he should have one mental group in which are found all object endings: if he must go mentally through 5 tables in order to gather them, he does not have the endings in the most efficient and workable form.

Hence, this text uses horizontal presentation of declensions. First the object endings are taught (the name objective is used to correlate with English classes—and "accusative" is really a mistranslation made by Roman grammarians of a Greek word; it should have been "causative case"). Meanwhile, the student is using subject endings and also ablatives: RECALL THAT PASSIVE MASTERY IS ENOUGH HERE. He need not be able to explain: it is enough at first to get the sense. This is easily possible. For the ablatives are all with prepositions and the word order at first is about the same as English. Next, the subject and the ablative are taught. This is done for three declensions at a time. Soon the 4th and 5th declensions are introduced. The dative and the possessive case are withheld for some time. They are less needed (Strain's study, cited above, shows that the ablative is almost four times as frequent in actual literature as the possessive), and it gives a large psychological advantage to have fewer endings at first, and to be able to learn the declensions of the most important pronouns on a three case system—it is easy later to present the possessives of all pronouns in one lesson, and the datives in another. Meanwhile, it is a great psychological advantage that the students need to face only a three instead of a five case table.

Learning Vocabulary: Due to the fact that the possessive case is not presented for some time, the ablative case is given as the second form in the vocabulary, to provide the stem. This means a slight inconvenience in the fifth declension, where the e overlaps with the e of third. The problem is solved by adding the number (5) with fifth declension words—and there are very few such words. But there is a considerable advantage in third declension. There the student is instructed to associate a possessive plural in -um and a neuter plural in -a with the ablative in -e of the vocabulary listing; while an -i in the vocabulary listing is to be associated with a possessive plural in -ium and a neuter plural in -ia. Since third declension adjectives also need the distinction of "i" and consonant stems, the ablative is listed with 3rd declension adjectives.

In listing verbs in the vocabulary, only three parts are given, e.g., amare, amavit, amatus. After all, the usual amo etc. can readily be formed from the infinitive. So there is no need to burden the memory and add to the psychological strain by calling for the memorizing of four parts where three will suffice. Only in the case of capio type verbs is there need for a listing of four parts: there we give a "preliminary" part, e.g., capiunt, ere, cepit, captus.

Teacher's Manual

There is no printed vocabulary in the back of the first year book: the idea is to require that the students make a vocabulary notebook. The notebook provides good practice, helps learning, and, because it is less convenient to use, encourages more memorizing. It is suggested that a loose leaf book be used, with one sheet for each letter. In addition, it is well to make three columns in each sheet, as is done in the first year book: left column for verbs, right for nouns and adjectives, middle for miscellaneous. Students can estimate space needed for future insertions. If space is lacking in the future, the sheet can be recopied—a very good exercise.

The chief method of learning vocabulary is the rereading mentioned above. A study by C. Handschin (*Methods of Teaching Modern Languages*, N.Y.. 1923, pp. 238-39) shows that when words are learned in context, students learn eight times as many words as when they are learned mechanically: the superiority is even greater after a lapse of time. As a supplement to this technique however, the students can use packs of cards: on each card is written one word, Latin on one side, English on the other. The student goes through the stack, making one pile for words he finds he knows, another for those he does not know. When he does not know a word, he looks at the other side for the answer. After going through the pack, he takes the pile of those not known and goes through again, and so on until he has given each word correctly.

As far as possible, we should try to teach the student to have the word <u>equus</u> associated not with the word horse, but with the concept. Some use of pictures can be made in the connection.

Latin by the Natural Method

We should stress the fact that if a student has to be weak on something, it is much better to be weak on forms etc.— anything but vocabulary.

<u>Teaching Gender</u>: The vocabulary listings for gender are in a different form. No gender is marked for declensions 1, 2, 4, 5. A general rule is given in lesson 11 for these, and easily suffices. Third declension gender is presented by <u>association</u>. Each noun in the vocabulary is accompanied by an adjective, whose form shows the gender, e.g., pes magnus. For the native speakers knew gender not by brute memory, but from hearing certain combinations occur frequently. It is another instance of automatic memory habits.

<u>Teaching constructions:</u> The more concrete the presentation, the better. It is best not to start with a rule, and then give examples. Rather, we should present examples first, and then generalize later. Students will learn more readily if they are taught to <u>compare a sentence to be translated with models in the book</u> (or still better, with memorized models) and to imitate these models, both for Latin to English and English to Latin. For example, in presenting the indirect statement with the objective-infinitive, the text will give a set of examples: let the student compare new sentences with these models and imitate them. Again, for conditional sentences, the text first shows bow to translate <u>if</u> sentences which use, in English, what seems to be indicative forms—merely use indicative in Latin too, with obvious tenses (the peculiarities of English use of present for future can be presented <u>after</u> the student has gone over the whole matter. Colloquial Latin in ancient times did often use present for future, just as English now

Teacher's Manual

does). As to the <u>if</u> sentences in which the English uses some special verb forms (note that it has <u>would</u> in the second part of the sentence,) these all have subjunctive—present at first by comparing with models in the text.

   <u>After</u> the student has become somewhat used to handling sentences by means of models, then it is profitable to give him a rule, and see that he understands it—but his chief tool in practice will still be the more or less automatic use of models. Note that the text commonly presents structures in the form of rules—the purpose is to give a clear statement for use after the presentation by models. But a teacher is needed to make the approach through models. The text is not intended for use without a teacher.

<u>The use of grammatical labels</u>: A certain amount of use of grammatical labels is good and cannot be avoided. But it is best kept at a minimum. The book cannot avoid using them, but the teacher can de-emphasise them as much as possible. Labels are not sufficiently concrete to be easily grasped—and they can easily come between two things that should be united. Thus, a student should have a direct mental connection between <u>amavit</u> and <u>he loved</u>. If a label "present perfect indicative active third singular of the verb meaning love" intervenes, it makes the process less direct and much more cumbersome. Actually, we aim to establish, so far as possible, an even more basic connection, so that the word <u>amavit</u> brings to mind not only not the label, but not even the English "he loved"; it should convey the idea itself directly. This process is more obvious in the matter of nouns than verbs. Thus <u>equus</u> should stand, not so much for the English word "horse" as for a *concept* of that animal. Rereading and oral Latin help much to establish this connection. Pictures would be valuable supplement.

Latin by the Natural Method

<u>Reviews</u>: It will be noted that every fourth lesson is a review. On no account should these lessons be omitted. The teacher may, of course, skip some of the suggested review drills, if the students have points they would like to review (and this is often the case). It is very good to sum up from time to time all of the verb forms had thus far, putting up a table on the board, and giving the English translation for each.

<u>Tests</u>: After each review lesson a test is planned. Chief stress should be placed on vocabulary. In vocabulary items, the teacher may give <u>any</u> of the parts of a word, and require the student to give the other parts and the meaning. In testing forms, the comments made above on labels should be noted. It is a useless strain to call for "perfect indicative active third singular, love" when one could just as well say: "he has loved". The class can be instructed that for test purposes, the most characteristic perfect translation is to be used: "he has loved", etc., and similarly for the imperfect: "he was loving". Where subjunctives are used, we may recall that most of the actual occurrences of subjunctives are translated as indicative e.g., this is true in result clauses, <u>cum</u> clauses, indirect questions, and in many conditions. Therefore for test purposes, the teacher can call for, e.g., "he was loving" (Subjunctive) and expect to get: <u>amaret</u> and vice versa.

Structures, prepositional uses, etc. can easily be tested by presenting complete sentences, either Latin to English or English to Latin, in which just a few words are underlined and are to be translated.

Teacher's Manual

Let us also recall at this point what was said above in the paragraph on presenting verb forms about the distinction of active and passive mastery on certain forms.

<u>Presenting case uses</u>: An unnecessary burden is usually placed upon the student in the elaborate classification of case uses and rules for prepositions. This is particularly true of the ablative. In actual practice, when a student sees an ablative, does he first classify and then get the sense, or vice versa? Obviously, he cannot classify until he has first gotten the sense. Hence, for Latin to English, classification is unnecessary. For English to Latin it is useful chiefly in deciding when to use prepositions. The rules ordinarily given are merely a description of the practice of Cicero. Now Latin came from Indo-European, a language in which there were no prepositions, the work being done by case endings instead. Latin developed into the Romance languages, in which case endings have almost disappeared, their function being taken over by prepositions. Latin itself is in an in-between position, having developed some uses of prepositions, and not others. The actual practice of Cicero (and, for that matter, of any good writer) is based on no rules of logic. It is merely a matter of what he, following <u>usage</u>, happened to use. In itself, it is neither good nor bad. The rules in Late Latin for prepositions happen to be much simpler. Therefore this text employs the Late Latin rules, which are given in the grammatical section of the second year book.

In the first year, only a very few rules are given. In the first lesson, students are taught to translate ablatives with prepositions. Soon ablatives without prepositions are presented, but then the student is not taught to classify, he is told merely to supply an English preposition: <u>in</u>, <u>by</u>, or

Latin by the Natural Method

<u>with</u>. Later in the year the text adds: <u>from</u> and <u>because of</u>. Late in the year a few rules are given for prepositions, chiefly the distinction of instrument and agent. Meanwhile, there is no problem in Latin to English; in English to Latin, the teacher can quietly correct mistakes (following the Late, not the Ciceronian rules), but will do well not to require any active mastery until the book presents certain rules.

<u>English to Latin:</u> Three sentences begin to appear in lesson 9; the number of sentences is soon raised to seven. The teacher may, if he wishes, correct papers as is commonly done. But this is not necessary, nor is it specially useful. Instead, a different method may be followed. If so, it is well to explain to the class what is being done and why.

If a student turns in sentences worth an A, the teacher cannot enter A in the grade book: he knows that probably the student has attained that degree of excellence only with the help of cooperation, and perhaps has merely copied. This cannot be prevented, and working together is even beneficial. But if a paper has sentences worth a D then the teacher knows that that student, probably even with help, could not produce work better than a D. He is justified in marking down a D, since the student is at least that poor.

Hence the teacher could give a poor grade, but could not give a good grade for a paper: the papers little certain information, only practice for the student. That practice can be had in a different way.

Let the students be told to write out their sentences and bring them to class. In class, four students will be sent to the board, to put up sentences 4, 5, 6, 7 (one each). While this is done, the class will cover the first three sentences orally. When the sentences have been written, the teacher will note in the grade book the fact that these students have

Teacher's Manual

been called, and may enter poor grades if he wishes, but not good ones, for the reasons just given. But the real information is obtained by observing correctors.

A student is appointed to correct sentence 4, either orally or at the board. In so doing, he is not permitted merely to compare it with his own paper: he must allow anything that is really correct in itself. The teacher, in watching and questioning the corrector, can see what he knows, and there is no fear of collaboration now. It is well for the teacher to refrain from indicating at this point whether or not the statements of the corrector are true: he should draw him out, at times, with questions but accept cheerfully any statement, however erroneous. When the corrector announces he has no further comments, then the teacher calls on the class as a whole (volunteers) to correct both the original and the corrections. (Further information on the students' knowledge is gained from hearing the volunteer corrections). Then the teacher does state clearly which solutions are correct, and discusses various possibilities. If some student has on hand a translation that has not been discussed, he is to raise his hand and ask about it.

In this process it is good, though not necessary, to have the corrector give his corrections in Latin, as far as he is able. The teacher similarly can give explanations in Latin (grammatical terms are easy to guess), but should, if it is anything other than simple matter, explain afterwards in English also. A few stock formulae will go very far: e.g.,"<u>paravet</u> debuit esse <u>paravit</u>", is a type of correction formula that applies to almost anything. When time is more crowded, as may easily happen in the later part of the year, it will be permissable to do more, or all, of the sentences orally.

Latin by the Natural Method

Private study rules for students: The chief instructions on how to prepare a translation passage have already been given above. The most essential feature to be stressed (and it will have to be done often, for it is hard to convince students of its need) is REREADING MANY TIMES. We might add a few miscellaneous suggestions here.

First of all, when a student, in his preparation, finds himself stalled on a sentence (which is not often in first year), let him be warned not to spend an inordinate amount of time on the one sentence. He may ask the help of other students, but if for any reason he does not get it, let him merely pass over that sentence and wait for it to become clear in class. If it should happen that he is called on for it in class, the teacher should accept the excuse (as long as it ii infrequent) that he was honestly stalled there. Then the teacher should call on some other student, and after that, make any needed explanations about the point that caused the difficulty. However, IT WOULD BE A GREAT MISTAKE TO CONSIDER A DIFFICULTY AS MERELY AN INTELLECTUAL PROBLEM TO BE CLARIFIED—to some extent it is that, and clarification is in order. But one must also remember that if the student had had a familiarity with that pattern of difficulty built up through linguistic habits, it would not have caused trouble. Therefore, it would be a great error merely to explain the difficulty and then drop the passage. The student who had trouble must reread that particular passage many times over, until it seems easy for him to follow it without translating. In that way he is building up a linguistic habit for dealing with that sort of pattern. The number of widely different patterns that can occur is limited. When one has "made friends" with a large number of such patterns, he will have a protection against such difficulties in the future. It is much like the case of a piano student who stumbles: if he merely plays on after a stumble, he does not develop, and will continue to stumble. But if instead he goes back and plays through the difficult measure many times, he develops habitual skills that will enable him easily to conquer similar difficulties in the future.

It is well, when the entire class finds a passage difficult, if the teacher will stop in class and after explaining the sense, reread the sentence aloud several times for the whole class.

Another good suggestion for private study is this: let the student not try to concentrate for more than 15-30 minutes at a time. Let him break his study periods sufficiently to remove fatigue. It is well to encourage students to make a block schedule of hours of the day for each day in the week, filling in the hours of classes and other necessary exercises, and also fixed study periods, well distributed and broken up.

Still another help, particularly in learning constructions, is for the student to see if he cannot find an easier way to summarize the rule than that which the book has. Sometimes he will find one, sometimes not, but the effort induces an excellent concentration that fixes facts well.

When he is in class, the student ought to recite silently with each one who recites. Thus his practice is multiplied by the number of students in the class.

Correcting errors: If a student translates Latin to English or English to Latin incorrectly, tell him what would be the Latin or English for the form he used. Do not say e.g., "You made it active and it should be passive," but tell him instead the Latin or English equivalent (as the situation require) of the form he gave.

Latin by the Natural Method

The problem of fear: Most students come to Latin class with a fear of the subject, usually acquired from listening to other students. A belief that he cannot learn it well or that it is terribly difficult is very harmful, and may set up a psychological block to learning.

There are many ways of dealing with this problem. For one thing, the text is paced very slowly at the start of the year, and the word order is very easy at first. This helps much.

A special device for combating fear is the use of humor. The text opens with "Mary had a little lamb" and "This little pig went to market". The lamb and the pigs are used for much nonsense, particularly in the first part of the book. Most of this is necessarily on a childish level: the forms. vocabulary etc. available preclude anything else. Later in the year, a normally good grade of joke replaces the earlier style of humor. Some of the better samples of jokes are found in lessons: 53, 59. 63, 65, 68, 74.

The teacher can help also by the use of "psychological crutches" while speaking Latin, as was explained above.

But the general attitude of the teacher is of the greatest importance. It is best to adopt an encouraging tone whenever it is possible—and that will be much of the time. There are, of course, off days, but even then it is helpful to comment calmly that "this must be an off day, and we have had and will get better days". Or again, the *"forsan et haec olim meminisse iuvabit"* approach is good: when something difficult comes up, as it must at times, let the teacher remind the class: "Do you remember how hard the agreement of adjectives seemed when we first met it? It seems easy now, doesn't it—this will soon seem just as easy." And of course, the teacher should slow down greatly

Teacher's Manual

at certain difficult points, such as agreement of adjectives, making more speed on the easier things.

<u>Quantity of matter to be covered in class:</u> All passages should always be read completely and at least six times by the students outside of class. But in class, when there is not time (and that will vary) it may be necessary to omit portions. The following treatment of the various passages is suggested:

1. The first story in each lesson is best covered by the oral question and answer method described above. it is not translated in class. It is easy to cover all of it by this method.

2. The "Nunc Exerceamus Nos" is best covered by fairly exact translation. Very early in the year, within a few lessons of the start, it is well to have the students close books for this passage. (In this section, some translation should also be done with books open. When time permits, it is well to cover it twice, once with books open, once with books closed. This will often be possible early in the year, less often later). Let the teacher read a sentence to be translated, then pick a student to translate it. At first sight, this method seems to be very difficult for students, but experience shows it is easier even for the weaker students. The teacher can modify the word order, making it easier for poor students, harder for the better students. He can also read in larger or smaller blocks (repeating, of course, on request), and can read at slower or faster rates of speed. In this way, the demands can be tailored to the ability of the student who is called on. If time does not permit taking all of this exercise, part can be omitted, but the class should never know in advance which part will be omitted, and the teacher should sometimes begin at the start, sometimes in

the middle, sometimes nearer the end, etc. Or, better, one may take the whole exercise and shorten the time by calling on students by name for part and accepting volunteers for the rest - further gain is had by not having them read the Latin aloud before translating during part of the Exerceamus.

3. The Scramble Exercise is very brief and can always be covered completely. Because of its difficulty, it is best to translate it exactly, with books open.

Supplementary reading: The students are to be encouraged to read Latin narratives in addition to the text (but discouraged from reading other elementary books during their first two years). It would be best to begin with the Gospels, then, selected narrative parts of Old Testament. The student may be encouraged to look up words freely in an English copy, provided he then rereads the same sentence. This supplementary reading could begin about midyear. A low price complete Latin Bible can be had from: Academy Library Guild, Box 549, Fresno, Calif. Ask for Biblia Vulgata Latina (cloth bound).

Teacher's Manual

III. SPECIFIC SUGGESTIONS FOR PRESENTING EACH LESSON

<u>Preliminary comments:</u> 1. The following are all mere suggestions. No two classes are entirely alike. Hence modifications will need to be made according to such differences. The teacher's ingenuity may suggest others. No pretense is made that any particular suggestion given here is the best possible way of presenting an item. In the interests of space and brevity, suggestions have been worded as though they were definite prescriptions. The teacher is asked to kindly excuse this style, realizing that space makes it necessary.

    2. In teaching vocabulary, some teachers, particularly in High Schools, will want to have a five minute vocabulary drill daily or with each lesson. It is good where desired or needed. Whether or not this is done, it is well to suggest to the students, in addition to the methods given above, that they make an original Latin sentence with each new vocabulary word. If so, it is probably best that up to lesson 10 they merely find one in the book, and afterwards, if they can, make their own,

    3. IT IS OF GREATEST IMPORTANCE TO KEEP THE COURSE MOVING ON SCHEDULE. Teachers accustomed to drill for complete active mastery will find previous habits make them disinclined to move on before attaining complete active mastery, and so will need to watch lest they slip into previous habits. Rate of speed will vary according to difficulty of matter. In general, it is good to take it a bit more slowly than average would require for first few

weeks, and to make up time later. Since various schools have various amounts of time available, flexibility is provided for: Class may stop anytime after lesson 64, and cover the omitted matter in 2nd year (see p. 28)

4. Do not forget to add the pattern practice to each lesson, and word order practice in lessons 20-28, 39-41, 51-52.

Comments on Individual Lessons

1. The psychological tone is of extreme importance in the beginning, to combat fear. A light, almost joking attitude (in so far as class discipline will allow) is good, to give the very true impression that this is not really hard (though neither is it mere play). On the first day, after assigning seats etc. begin at once with *Maria habuit parvum agnum*, without any preparation or explanation. Have them translate with books open. Read the sentence to them in Latin—have them repeat before translating. No need to teach pronunciation separately. It is best to have a short lesson on the first day, going over merely the Maria and the Columbus stories. But explain also the student study procedure at some length (cf. the general suggestions). Stress that if they will reread, they will gain FAR more than if not. Urge, then, to learn to follow without translating. Demonstrate that they can do it, after they have gone over the first selection, by reading it slowly to them several times. Tell them that the English words will stick in their minds for some time even when they try to do without them—do not be discouraged: you will get over that gradually. Remember, little Roman morons—so high, could do it—they did not translate into Swiss. Do not give the grammar explanation, nor ask to read with books closed, nor use oral questions on the first day. On the second day,

Teacher's Manual

go over these same passages again, with books open. Then ask questions, with books open, (See the samples on [page number] 27). Give them a sample of how to answer before starting. Urge them to try not to translate your questions; remember the little Roman moron! Then, if time permits have them close books, and translate the same passage again from your reading. On second day, go over the grammar lightly. Tell them you will explain about a vocabulary notebook on the next day. Translate the "Columbus and Lamb stew", first with books open, then with them closed.

2. Put on board samples of how to enter words in a vocabulary notebook. The book should be large, loose-leaf and one sheet for each letter. Try to gauge space for insertion of new words. If the sheet gets too crowded, recopy. Use three columns like the text does. Samples: agnus_____ - lamb. Tell them to leave a blank (it will hold the abl. sg. and, for 3rd decl., also an adjective to show gender) between the noun and its meaning. Similarly for adjectives: planus_____ - flat

Miscellaneous words go in second column. Enter them just as they are in the vocabulary. (Can add cases taken by preps. later). Verbs thus: _____, dedit, _____- gave. Tell them there will be two more parts, somewhat as English verbs have parts (do not elaborate). It is good to make these notebooks even though there is now a vocabulary in the back of the book.

Then translate the 5 pigs and the Romulus & Remus with books open. After that, ask oral questions. Then close the books, and translate by ear. Next go over the grammar and vocabulary with them. Ordinarily this should be done the day before taking the first readings of a given lesson.

Latin by the Natural Method

Then with books open, read "A Bit More Stew". Always let them read the Latin before translating (when books are open) in the exercise section. It is not necessary for the teacher to read it first after the 1st day, but the teacher should correct their mispronunciations. Next close books and translate it by ear. For a few lessons, in so far as time permits, it is good to cover the first passage, first by oral questions, then close books and translate it by ear. If there is not time for both, the oral questions alone will suffice. On the exercise, translate with books open, then with books closed. When time does not permit, do it only with books closed. It is not necessary to cover all of the <u>Exerceamus</u> in each lesson. Point out also that <u>dixerunt</u> without a word like <u>Romani</u> ahead of it will mean "they said". Give a few other examples, but do not dwell long on it. (As to the Roman history in this and following lessons, it is on the whole accurate and authentic. The only exception is for the insertion of a very few legends from Roman writers themselves, particularly where, as in the royal period and expulsion of kings, the exact facts cannot be found at present—the truth on Tarquin is vague, and the story of Hortius is probably legend).

3. Procedure in general is as outlined above, but in the grammar section, go back through all previous vocabularies and ask the students to give abl. sg. for all nouns thus far. Let them associate the -a abl. sg. with objective -am etc. If they have trouble, supply it for them, and do not press the point, for the fact of the existence of several declensions is barely dawning on them. It will become clearer in lesson 5. For the distinctions of cases with prepositions, have them go back and use each preposition with each noun in all vocabularies thus far. For <u>in</u>:

Teacher's Manual

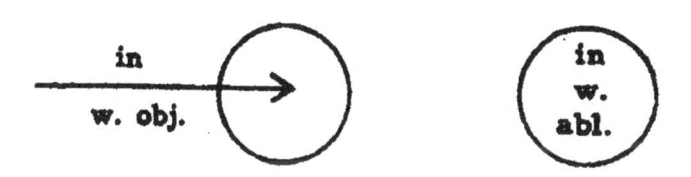

Encourage students to learn cases with prepositions, not by memorizing: "*cum* takes abl.", but by memorizing a phrase with it: e.g., "*cum agno*". Urge them to make up their own sentences, in private for this. Do not drill this at this point—it would be too much active mastery at the present.

4. In general, every 4th lesson is a review. In place of the drill matter given in such lessons, it is good to invite the class to call for points on which they want special review, by the teacher, on the board. If time permits, both board review and the printed drills may be used. Not much drill on case endings should be done at this point, for they do not yet know the distinction of declensions (comes in lesson 5). Drill only a few of the more familiar words, such as agnus, nauta, rex. Drill only in sentences: e.g., Marcus vidit Do not spend too much time, nor insist much on it. At about this time, when reading the Exerceamus to the class with their books closed, one may begin to experiment cautiously with the word order, beginning it on some of the better students. That is, sometimes use, in simple sentences only, the Maria agnum habet word order. Do not say you will do it, nor comment (unless asked)—just do it. And throughout the year, much can be done by judiciously varying the word order when reading to the class—make it harder for better students (and faster and in larger blocks)—and easier (and in smaller blocks and slower) for poorer students. Teach the position of enim by using the Exerceamus of III; have them insert enim in a large number

Latin by the Natural Method

of sentences. The class after finishing each review lesson should have an exam. On the day before the exam put up some samples on the board of the manner in which to answer. The exams given herewith may be used. It makes it easier to correct if students write the question for each item. Working time allowed should be 20-25 minutes for exams at this point. That gives time to cover other things in the same period. Next day bring back graded papers, without writing out right forms for errors. Read off correct answers. Both teacher and pupil should note what sort of things were missed, and give special attention to those things.

5. The Secession story in this chapter is from Livy and is also historicity doubtful. Stress the function of the ablative (cf. theory above, 10). Go back with the class over all previous vocabularies and ask them to give the abl. of each noun—when they cannot reasonably be expected to guess, tell them. And ask them to put abl. In their notebooks. Also ask them to tell the decl. of each noun from ablative. Draw up samples on the board thus:

| puell | puella
am
a
as
is | agn | agnus
um
o
os
is | reg | rex
em
e
es
ibus |

Do not extend the line to the nom. Singular tell them it does work many times, but it is not dependable, therefore, we do not do it. Get a few students to put up similar

Teacher's Manual

schemata on board for practice. Show the class where to put the new forms in blanks provided.

    6. In teaching the nom. pl. again put up diagrams on the board as in 5, and add the nominative forms. Note especially <u>vir</u> and <u>ager</u>.

    7. Do not bother much with adjectives used as nouns today—that will come up again later in connection with gender, and can be understood better then. But this helps prepare the way. Give a few examples, without stress, at this time: <u>boni</u>, <u>mali</u>, <u>parvi</u>, <u>magni</u>. Better not give neuter examples now. In presenting the new case endings, have the class compare them to endings they already know and announce their results. This is regularly a good procedure in introducing new tables and it helps the memory. But warn them they still need much practice.

<u>Ablatives without prepositions:</u> Stress that there are 2 kinds of abls.: 1. with prepositions 2. Without prepositions For 1—just translate the prepositions For 2—must supply one—in, by, with (there will be two more later: from, because of). Let general sense tell which to supply. Drill this by means of the <u>Exerceamus</u> of this lesson. Add others at will. Be sure to cover the <u>Exerceamus</u> twice in this lesson (books open and closed). The <u>Exerceamus</u> of VIII also has many examples of abl. without preps.

    8. If students wish to review something other than matter given, that is to be preferred. If not, review declensions on the board. In 5 we had some drill in vertical fashion on noun endings. Now we should drill horizontally. Put up 5 nouns. Ask someone to give orally all the objectives (or let one give sgs. another pls.). Do it with two or three sets of nouns. Use sentences like <u>Marcus vidit</u>, as in

Latin by the Natural Method

4, for drill. Encourage students to do more of the same privately, and explain why horizontal drill is practical (cf. theory p. 9). But urge them to practice privately also vertically (though lese). Admit some may find one way more helpful than others—but most will find horizontal best. It is well to speak part of the time of nominatives as "subject endings" and objectives as "object endings".

9. Tell them that an infinitive is simply the Latin way of saying "to love, to hear", etc. Just as an English verb has three parts—do, did, done, etc., so Latin has three parts. We must now learn two parts. Call attention to the 4 different inf. Endings—say we will see later what they are good for. Make no special point of them now, AND DO NOT MENTION CONJUGATIONS. In presenting the new endings on the board, add up also all old endings. Point out the endings that have several possibilities thus:

4.	5.
us us	es es
us	es

Be satisfied with little active control of 4th declension at present, and still less on 5th. And do not expect them to identify forms by name at present. Drill should be in the concrete form of sentences, as explained above in chapters 4 and 8. Now the English to Latin sentences begin. Explain to the students the proper procedure, as explained in the general principles above, and tell them the reasons why this different procedure is bring used. Have them put up the three sentences, and appoint correctors as explained above.

Teacher's Manual

When they make a mistake on the matter of using or omitting prepositions with ablative, tell them the right usage, but make no point of it, and do not deduct for it—for only much later will that be presented. Meanwhile, no harm will be done, and they will not make too many errors when measured by the Late Latin rules (see the summary in the second year book pp.153-54). But it is good to take this opportunity for some drill on endings. For that, use a blank sentence: Marcus vidit_____. Tell them now we wish to fill in that blank with quite a number of things: lamb, lambs, land, lands, queen, queens, pig, pigs, man, men, field, fields, army, armies, sailor, sailors, king, kings, city, cities, law, laws, power, powers, ship, ships. To practice the ablative, use two blank forms, according to the required sense: Marcus venit cum_____. Marcus fuit in_____. Again, use the above list of nouns for the blanks. To practice the nominative use _____ est (sunt) in urbe Romana. Do not expect perfection or fluency from them in this. They have had little in the exactness of English-Latin at this point. Tell them that we will need to practice on this privately too—and that it will grow gradually with them. As long as they can make passing grades on exams of the type given in this manual and can do well with English to Latin sentences on the board, the degree of active mastery is sufficient for the time being. Actually, they have a larger load of declension forms than is usual at this time of the year—but do not tell them that. Explain how to make cards for private practice. On one side put the sentence with the question: Marcus vidit (a lamb). On other side the answer: Marcus vidit agnum. Let them make cards, shuffle, try to answer. If in doubt or do not know, look at other side. Put cards into two piles—one of those known, one of those not known, until all are covered. Then go though the not

Latin by the Natural Method

known pile again, and so on until there are none left that are not known. At first, keep objectives together etc., then later mix). If tapes are available, put these drills on tape thus: Marcus vidit—pause—agnum. Student should answer during the pause, then listen to the answer on the tape.

Put up a schema on the board for each of three nouns: <u>bellum</u>, <u>mare</u>, <u>nomen</u>. With <u>bellum</u>, put up <u>agnus</u>. Point out that actually there is not much new in bellum. Circle the endings that are new. Draw a tie line from the nom. to the obj. endings, both singular and plural. Tell them all neuter nouns in Latin (and in Greek, if you wish too) are same in subject and object endings, and that their plurals are all in -a (some in -ia as we will see). All of the neuters in the second declension follow bellum. Put up <u>nomen</u>, parallel to <u>rex</u>, and point out as for <u>agnus</u>-<u>bellum</u>. DO NOT EXPLAIN WHAT NEUTER GENDER MEANS, AND DO NOT USE THE WORD GENDER—just speak of neuters, or neuter nouns. How to tell which have -<u>ia</u> instead of just –<u>a</u>? In second declension, it has -<u>ia</u> if the first form has -<u>ium</u>. In third, it has -<u>ia</u> if the ablative is in -<u>i</u>—other wise just -<u>a</u>. Stress this simple means. Do not press them to learn the <u>n</u>, <u>t</u>, <u>men</u>, <u>ma</u>, etc. rule.

11. This lesson requires special care: *spend about three days on it.* There is no other part of the first year book that will *appear* as difficult to the students. They will make wholesale mistakes; even the better students will make many. Do not register dismay, but be calm, take an encouraging but realistic attitude. Tell them they will find it a bit hard, but only temporarily. In a few weeks they will be able to look back and wonder why it seemed so hard. And teachers accustomed to drilling for full active mastery at once in traditional methods must take care not to be

Teacher's Manual

discouraged themselves. They need to realize that *students now have on hand the greater part of all five declensions*; much more than traditional books have at this point. So one must not expect too much. Furthermore, the very notion of agreement is something completely strange to them. Hence anything like real active mastery is simply not to be hoped for at present. But the experience of many teachers shows that by following directions carefully, and avoiding too much insistence on active mastery, students will get over this hump very well. Explain first that while English calls nouns masc. fem., or neuter according to real sex, Latin ordinarily does not bother about real sex. Just as English speaks of a ship as a "she", so Latin uses artificial gender for all nouns. Go over the rules for the several declensions. Tell them they need to learn gender from vocab. only for 3rd decl. nouns. The "hand rule" is very helpful. Hold up hand, count fingers: 1, 2, 3, 4, 5, starting from little finger, then starting from thumb. In either direction, it ends (1 or 5 depending on which end one starts with) with a feminine. Next fingers (2 & 4) will be mostly masc., though with some neuters. the middle (3) has all three. Now write up a table of bonus on the board. Mark in large letters M. F. N. over the proper columns. Give a few examples of agreement from the Exerceamus. Point out: there are three facts about each: 1. Is it masc. fem., or neut.? 2. Is it singular or plural? 3. Is it subject or object ending or ablative? (Note the avoidance of the terms: gender, case, number. As much as possible, be concrete. Many will not answer if you ask: What gender? But will answer if you may "Is it masc., fem., or neuter?") Then go through the rest of the Exerceamus, making them give the same three facts about every pair. Next, drill with the following material; expend almost two full periods on it. Use the blank sentences of lesson 9. Let the teacher give the

Latin by the Natural Method

Latin noun, have a student add any adjective: Marcus vidit agnum _____. A good lamb, the good lambs (make each one first s.g. then plural), a great land, a great queen, the bad pig, a good man, a good field, a great army, a great war, a great danger, the good sailor, a good king, a large city, a good law, a good name, a large sea. great power, a good ship. Insist that they give the noun first—it is easier, for the adj. agrees with it, not vice-versa. Again, in talking about gender, avoid using the word "gender" very much—instead say: Is it masc., fem., or neuter? For the ablative, use one of the following blanks, according to sense, with the same list of phrases as above: Marcus venit cum_____. Marcus fuit in _____ _____.

For drilling nominative use: _____est (sunt) in urbe Romana. It is not necessary, of course, that you or they repeat the other words of the sentence with each example, though it may be done. Do not be surprised at the fact that they will have trouble even with the nom. sg. They are not yet used to precision and active mastery. It must come very gradually, as a long range project. To drive home the fact that eat takes no object, and for additional drill, use the following blank, and tell them to fill in any adjective they wish: Agnus est _____. Terra est _____.

Use both sg. and pl. The teacher gives the first two words, using up all nouns in the above list. Again, as in lesson 9, urge them to make cards to practice with privately, unless two work together. They then can work from a list. If tapes are available, record the above drills, leaving a pause thus: Marcus vidit agnum, good—pause—<u>bonum</u>. Student should answer during pause, then listen to answer on tape. If they can answer even fairly well in exams of the types given in this manual, and can do English to Latin sentences fairly well, they have attained

Teacher's Manual

enough in this respect for the present. However, keep an eye on this matter on the long range to be sure they improve. If sharpening is needed, such drills can be repeated later (not too many of them). And the inclusion of such Items in tests will help.

12. If drilling indicated above has been done, probably little additional drill will be needed with the review—the small amount given in the book will probably suffice.

13. Put up in parallel columns on the board, the declension of <u>fortis</u>, compared to <u>civis</u> and <u>mare</u>. Stress again the peculiarities of all neuters and note the ablative in -<u>i</u> on adjectives; tell them just a few have abl. in -e, but they will be listed as such in the vocabulary. Next put up <u>acer</u>, on another part of board, leaving the first tables up. *But do not write in <u>acris</u> at first (though leave a small space for it).* Write it the same as <u>fortis</u>. Then, when that is well enough understood, write up <u>acris,</u> and put a ring around it—tell them <u>acer</u> is same as <u>fortis</u> but for that one form—the nom. s. fem.—e.g., Maria fuit acris. How can you tell when an adj. will behave like acer? Look at the vocabulary listings. Next do a bit of drill. You should probably use only the objective case, with the form: Marcus vidit, as in lesson 11. Use the following list (singular and plural of each item): a brave king, a sharp citizen, a brave lamb, a brave pig, a sharp war, a sharp sea, a brave army, a brave man, a sharp sailor. During the drill, leave the tables on the board, and invite them to use them if needed. Then, if space permits, leave the tables on the board (at least <u>fortis</u>) and write up <u>ferox</u> in two complete columns. Get certain ones in the class to figure out what the forms should be. With the help of the neuter rules, this can be done. Next, drill with the following

51

Latin by the Natural Method

blank: Marcus vidit _____ (use singular and plural for each) a fierce king, citizen, lamb, pig, war, sea, army, man, sailor.

Then, drill again with the following three blanks: Marcus vidit _____. Marcus venit cum _____ (or: fuit in) _____. Rex fuit (reges fuerunt) _____ (etc., with the various nouns). Use the following list with the singular and plural of each item:

a brave king   a fierce sea
a sharp citizen   a sharp army
a fierce lamb   a brave man
a brave pig   a sharp sailor
a sharp war

It is well to spend about a period and a half in all on such drilling. After this drilling is completed, take up the pluperfect tense. Stress the approach of: How do we say: "He had loved," etc. Do not place much stress on adjectives used as nouns at present. It will be well to run a bit below the average speed of 3 lessons per week for a time now, to allow for digestion of the principles of agreement and also of the passive voice and participles which are coming. However teachers accustomed to demanding complete active mastery in teaching traditional methods will need to watch themselves lest they fear to go ahead at these points when active mastery is far less than what they have been accustomed to demanding.

14. In the vocabulary, note especially <u>insidiae</u>, which has only plural, Ask class to find some English examples like it (e.g., scissors, pants; the latter is singular at top, plural at bottom). In presenting the passive, some care is needed.

Teacher's Manual

Best to use more than one presentation, to allow for individual differences. Most students should get it most easily by having a pattern to compare to.

vicit	he conquered	victus est	he was conquered
	he did conquer		he has been conquered
	he has conquered		

Insist that they compare new examples with this pattern and memorize the equivalents. This is easier than to try to get across the idea: In the active the subject acts while in the passive the subject is acted upon. It is well to mention that too—but it is abstract—and things stick best in the concrete. Before going ahead with any further points, or before explaining the gender differences in these forms, turn to the table of verbs in this lesson, and have a short drill; acceptus est, amatus est, etc., running around the class with it. After that, point out that victus behaves like bonus. So, we can say: victi sunt. Ask a few students to translate such forms. Then point out that, since victus is like bonus, we can also change it to mean: she was conquered, it was conquered. In the list, they will ask about the forms with the *. Tell them briefly these are future active participles, for verbs that have no perfect passive participles. But they are not supposed to know this now, so tell them "If you are curious: casurus means 'about to, going to, intending to fall'; futurus, 'about to, going to, intending to be'; osurus, 'about to, going to, intending to hate,' etc." Students, like other people, are just perverse enough to want to learn something when they shouldn't. Many will learn it this way; but do not place any stress on it. Point out also on the list the stock patterns, -are, -avit, -atus, etc. Note also that

53

Latin by the Natural Method

there really is not much to memorize as they already should know three of the four columns—and they will be asked to learn the extra parts of only 17 in next lesson, the rest in lesson after that. A normal vocabulary contains more words than that, when one adds up the several parts to be learned. So this is a good breather—and it gives us extra practice on the agreement matter. Recognizing familiar patterns -<u>avit</u>, -<u>atus</u> further reduces the load. There really isn't much work and it is there! Then take up participles as adjectives, giving a few examples, such as those in the book. Add also: Marcus vidit milites captos (just the same structure as if it were: bonos). Marcus venit cum militibus captis.

14. As we explained in Part II it is good to begin early in the year to summarize some previous parts of the story in your own words in Latin before beginning the oral question period. Lesson 14, or thereabouts, is a good time to begin. Here is a sample of how it might be done (should take 5 minutes, perhaps a little more). Explain to the class why you are doing it. Tell them if you go too fast to put up a hand. Tell them also they need not follow everything at once—it is good enough to follow snatches, and, if one holds on to them, the snatches will grow in size. It really will be fun. And more people speak than read any given language anyway. Be sure to have a map or two open at all times for this section—a good psychological crutch (cf. p. 8 above)—and point at it as often as possible, indicating places: In primus diebus, Romani habuerunt multa bella. Tarquinius fuit rex malus. Tarquinium expulerunt. Ergo Etrusci pugnaverunt contra Romanos. Sed etiam pugnaverunt contra Aequos. Vicerunt Aequos. Etiam pugnaverunt cum Carthagine. Carthago est in Africa septentrionali—non in Africa meridionali. Carthaginienses

non amaverunt pugnare. Carthagines boni mercatura fuerunt. Ergo multas naves habuerunt. In primo bello Punico, in primis diebus, Romani non habuerunt multas naves. Sed fecerunt multas naves. Consules Romani miserunt multos viros in naves. Carthaginienses non habuerunt multos milites in navibus. Ergo Romani potuerunt vincere Carthaginem in primo bello Punico. Post hoc bellum, Carthago dedit multum aurum. Ergo Carthaginienses voluerunt aurum rursus accipere. Imperator Carthaginiensis, Hamilcar, venit in Hispaniam. In Hispania fuit aurum multum. Hamilcar fuit imperator bonus. Cum Hamilcare venit puer parvus, Hannibal. Hamilcar fuit pater Hannibalis. Fabula Romana dixit quod Hannibal posuit manum in altari (gesture at desk) et promisit odium aeternum contra Romanos. In Hispania fuit urbs magna, Saguntum. Saguntini amaverunt Romanos. Et Romani amaverunt Saguntum. Sed Hannibal voluit capere Saguntum. Hannibal misit exercitum contra Saguntum. Saguntini miserunt legatos in senatum Romanum. Legati rogaverunt senatum mittere auxilium. Romani miserunt legatos in senatum Carthaginiensem. Legati dixerunt: Necesse est revocare Hannibalem. Sed Carthago non revocavit Hannibalem. Ergo Romani bellum fecerunt. Hannibal cepit Saguntum. Sed non remansit in Hispania.

Venit trans montes Pyrenaeos in Galliam. Romani exercitum miserunt in Galliam. Valuerunt pugnare cum Hannibale in Gallia. Sed non potuerunt pugnare cum Hannibale in Gallia Quia Hannibal in Gallia non remansit. Hannibal venit ex Gallia trans Alpes in Italiam. In exercitu Punico etiam elephanti fuerunt.

Now begin the usual questions for the story of lesson 14. Such continuous narratives as this need not always be of

Latin by the Natural Method

such length—and, strictly speaking, they would not have to be done with every lesson. But it is recommended to use them every few lessons, at least. In going back over the same matter, small variations in language can be used, e.g., in the next lesson, one may go over much the same matter, but using more of the passive forms introduced in 14. He may also go into more detail on the later phases of the story just before today's episode.

15 & 16. Stress today that the students should not take advantage of the lack of new matter to loaf—for there is not much work in getting up those 17 parts, but should use it to practice on anything that might not have been well digested thus far.

17. Stress that the ablative absolute is quite a convenience. Explain the name LIGHTLY—it is called "ablative" because it is in the ablative, and "absolute", because of no grammatical connection; but you should only mention this last, and place no stress on it at all for the moment. Then put the example given (or a similar one) on the board.

<u>Rege expulso</u>, Romani pugnaverunt.

The <u>king</u>, <u>HAVING BEEN</u> expelled, the Romans fought.

Draw arrows to show first the way to translate <u>rege</u>, then for <u>expulso</u>. Point out that it is only a crude starting translation. But insist on always using it until they get well accustomed to the abl. abs.—explain that will prevent their batting wildly. Then ask them (without calling attention to the expanded translations in the book) to think how they

Teacher's Manual

could express the same idea in English in a fuller way, in other words. Probably two or three or more offers will come, very free. Accept them as long as they are merely the same general thought. Then, turn to the list of expanded translations in the book and point out the possibilities there. Next, even if the previous lesson has not been finished (for *one should always look over the next lesson on the day before it comes up, even if not everything in the previous lesson has been covered*) have them turn to the Exerceamus. No need for them to have prepared it. Call on students to translate a sentence each. If they hesitate in translation, make them compare it with the example on the board, and model their translation on it. First let them give the crude translation, then 2 or 3 expanded forms. Go through the entire Exerceamus that way (on next day go over it again, preferably with books closed). On the first day, do not mention the problem of English—Latin abl. abs. Save that for the next class. Then, in that next class, point out that one can easily reverse the process, i.e., if one has a sentence containing one of the expanded forms (i.e., a clause with because, when, etc.) first try to convert it to the "king having been expelled" pattern. But now, for the absolute aspect of the structure, tell them to make a test: Look at the noun (e.g., the king)—see if it means the same person or thing as the subject or object of the rest of the sentence. If yes, we must not use the absolute. If no, we go ahead in the obvious way. Demonstrate one on the board for them. Then add a few other examples of your own. The English to Latin sentences of this lesson will show if it has been handled well (and the next test will also show it). One could, if desired, refrain from giving the test mentioned above on whether or not an absolute is possible. For the

Latin by the Natural Method

Eng. - Latin sentences given will not make it necessary to use it for some time.

18. Put on the board first: Mary's lamb—the lamb of Mary.
These are the same. How do we say it in Latin? Mariae agnus will do for both. Since it shows possession, we call it possessive case. Then put up the sample forms. Bring out the relation to the ablative in 3rd decl. Best to put very little stress on participles used as nouns, for the present time.

19 - 28. We now enter a very easy stretch of lessons. There is hardly anything in this series that should cause the students much difficulty. This is done to allow them to recover from the matter of agreement and absolutes which they have just faced. Point out to them that we now have an easy stretch, and why. But stress that nothing in the entire year will hit them so hard as the agreement did. Some things will be harder than the present stretch, but not too much harder. This is a good psychological tactic. For each of the new form tables of this section, put up the new table on the board, if you wish, or else have them open the book to that point. Better to write it up. Have the class look over each table and try to find a way to compare it to previous forms so as to see what is alike as well as what is different. Let them study it silently a few minutes until someone puts up a hand. Then, if the table is on the board, put a ring around the forms that one could not guess, that are completely new. Stress how few they are, how most of it is like bonus etc. A few specific comments follow:

19. Point out the shift—<u>that</u>, <u>those</u>. Note also the different uses of <u>ille</u> as substantive and as adjective.

Teacher's Manual

20. In declining words together, call for horizontal work: nom. sg. & pl., poss. sg.&pl. etc. If time permits, also do vertical work on the same combinations. The new word order is not entirely new—we have used some of it. And you probably have arranged still more, as the class can take it, in reading to them with their books closed and with oral questions in Latin. Point out that fact to them. It is very important to learn to follow without rearranging. They have already done some, probably. Read <u>Maria agnum habet</u> and a few other three word sentences aloud 6 times to them to demonstrate this fact.

21. In the pluperfect passive, at first do not begin with the label "pluperfect". Put on the board the equation:

                       victus erat = he had been conquered.
Compare it to   victus est = he has been conquered.

Make the direct connection between <u>victus erat</u> and <u>he had been conquered</u>. Do not let them first say: "Victus erat is pluperfect passive. The pluperfect passive of conquer in English is: He had been conquered". This puts an unnecessary, clumsy step between the Latin form and English equivalent (or mental comprehension). Place little stress on the label. But do point out the difference: <u>Victus erat</u> is one notch farther back in the past than victus est. In fact, it is always earlier in time to the main verb in the sentence.

Place little stress on <u>suus</u> now. Complete mastery would be a strain. They will readily handle the examples. Try just a few varied examples on the board.

Maria habuit agnum suum . . . . HER lamb.
Marcus habuit pecuniam suam . . . . HIS money.
Romani habuerunt leges suas . . . . THEIR laws.

Point out that the translation of <u>suus</u> is regulated by the subject. For, it reflects and to reflect, one must be away from the subject. The subject does not reflect on itself.

Mention the <u>eius</u> and <u>eorum</u> lightly and tell them they need not learn it now; we are just showing it for the sake of curiosity.

22. The present should cause little if any difficulty. Put up a series of infinitives on the board:

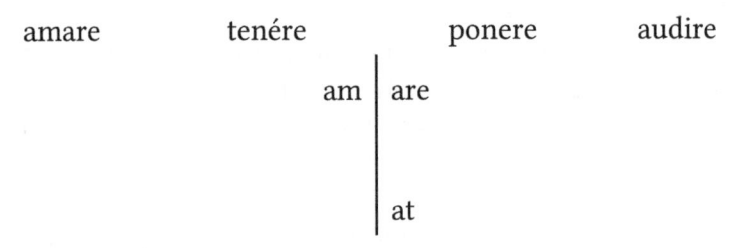

amare   tenére   ponere   audire

am | are

    | at

Point out that they all end in <u>t</u> but the vowel ahead varies, it will be the same as in the infinitive except for <u>ponere</u>. (Place no stress on the fact of conjugations today—just mention lightly that they are different series, just as nouns have different series of endings. Tell them that it makes a difference only on forms made from infinitive—not on other parts of verb). But suggest strongly that they memorize one sample of each kind—necessary to know how to draw the lines, but that is too cumbersome in practice. They must be able to give forms rapidly. It is much easier to imitate a set that one knows. As to meaning, again draw the same sort of direct connection as in 21:

amat means: he loves,
he does love
he is loving

Teacher's Manual

If they memorize one example, it will be easy.

23. Put up a set of samples as in previous lesson. May include <u>capiunt</u> in first set or add it later. No special trouble should be had. As to velle, explain we shall pick up a few forms at a time for a while as it is much easier than to face a lot-at once. Later we will have a lesson to sum them all up.

25. Note the difference between "there" as translated by <u>ibi</u> and "there" the expletive. Use two sentences: There were kings in Roman land. The kings were there. In the second "there" really means " in that place", and hence is <u>ibi</u>. In the first, "in that place" would be out of place. On <u>is</u> and <u>idem</u> have the class discover for themselves the resemblances to <u>bonus</u>. Give a few examples to show meaning of <u>is</u>: Marcus vidit eam - Marcus vidit eum - Marcus vidit id; Marcus vidit eos (eas) (ea). These are common but Marcus vidit eum agnum—is rare. Explain the purpose of the Scrambles, as given in the theory pages above. Note that each of the three kinds has its own value, like different kinds of vitamins. It is not enough to take one kind of vitamin (the best kind), and skip the others. When beginning this Scramble for the first time (and similarly when other specially hard new things come) call first for volunteers, or call on a few of the best students, to make it go smoothly at the start and minimize fear.

26. For declension of the relatives, have them go through and compare to known endings. Then, get them to translate some relatives BEFORE explaining about agreement of antecedents. Go through the <u>Exerceamus</u> with books open, even though lesson 25 has not been finished. Then, on next day, do it again with books closed. On the

second day, put up a few examples of relatives, and demonstrate the agreement, e.g., Maria, quam Marcus amat, est in schola.

Draw arrows to indicate quam is feminine and singular because of Maria—"the word to which it refers" (use "antecedent" less frequently, but sometimes). But note quam is objective because it is the object in its own clause. Suggest an optional checking method, then change the "who" in English to the proper form of he, she, it, they, and if need be, change the word order to see the function of the relative in its own clause, e.g., Mary— Marcus loves her—is in school.

27. Dwell little on quidam and certus. The declension of ipse and se is no great trouble. For their uses put a few samples on the board:

Caesar himself killed him. Caesar ipse interfecit eum. Caesar killed himself. Caesar interfecit se. Caesar killed him himself. Caesar ipse interfecit eum. Caesar himself killed himself. Caesar ipse interfecit se.

Urge them to almost memorize a few examples like these as it is easier to handle the distinction concretely, rather than by semi-abstract rules. Point out that the difficulty does not come in Latin to English, but in English to Latin. Then point out on the above examples, the principle: The reflexive has two characteristics and it must have both, one is not enough:

1) It is not part of subject.

2) It refers back to subject (reflects)—or, means same person or thing as subject.

If you wish, bring out also such an example as this. He killed Caesar himself.

Note the two possible meanings for himself, and the two translations accordingly. But in general, little stress and

Teacher's Manual

drill on <u>ipse</u> and <u>se</u> is needed, and little is advised at this time. Latin to English is no problem. English to Latin troubles can be handled, without too much stress, as they come up in the sentences from day to day.

29. Be sure to stress that <u>vincit</u> means: he conquers, he does conquer, he is conquering; while <u>vincitur</u> means: he is conquered, he is being conquered. It is much easier for them to grasp that than to use the almost abstract principle: in the active, the subject acts, in the passive, he is being acted upon. Follow similar procedure in all presentation of new verb forms.

30. Stress the learning of a pair of examples, such as those given, to make clear the kind of *to* or *for* translated by dative. Need not be really memorized, but should be close to it. Take the **Exerceamus** with book open, to facilitate getting used to new word order; then, if time permits, with book closed (at least apart of it).

31. For the towns and cities rule, use concrete approach, with a pair of examples: Discessit Roma. Discessit ex urbe. Venit Romam. Venit ad urbem.

33. Urge class to learn a set of models for imperfect, rather than learning a rule (too slow and clumsy: <u>amabat</u>, <u>tenebat</u>, <u>ponebat</u>, <u>capiebat</u>, <u>audiebat</u>. Five words is less work than a rule, and it is easier to imitate them than to apply a rule. Do similarly with other new verb forms. Put the four translations on the board, draw bracket on both sides—3 for perfect, 3 for imperfect.

34. Give a sample verb with the translations for the passive: he was loved, he was being loved. Cf. remarks on lesson 29 above. Put up a few samples of distinction of <u>suus</u> and <u>eius</u>—do not spend a lot of time on it; practice in reading will easily take care of it.

35. Put up a set of samples of present participles—urge to learn them rather than a rule (cf. comments on 33). Lay little stress on the difference between gerund and participle— it must clear slowly with experience. But stress that: AS TO USE, THE USES OF THE PRESENT PARTICIPLE ARE PARALLEL IN EVERY WAY TO THOSE OF THE PERFECT, the only DIFFERENCE IS THAT HERE WE USE THE ____-ING TRANSLATION, WHILE THERE WE HAD THE "HAVING BEEN". If you wish, give a few examples of participles in possessive and dative, but lay no stress on them if you use them at all.

37 - 38. Cf. remarks on lesson 29.

39. Put the four pattern sentences on the board. Comment on the occasional looseness in English on examples 3 and 4. Point out that there is no Latin word for that in this structure. Point out that the subject is in the objective case—quite illogically, but usage, not logic, rules language. Comment that the verb turns infinitive—equally illogical. Do not at first explain that "present infinitive indicates time going on relative to the main verb." Instead, insist that they work by comparing with examples. It is important that in making the comparison, they start by comparing the tense of the dicit, dixit etc., and only after that compare the subordinate clause. This will make it easier. Take at once the Exerceamus. Do not give any indication that this is a difficult structure; it is not, if correctly presented. Insist, however, in Latin - English translation that they always USE THE WORD "THAT" IN ENGLISH, for the first two or three weeks. It helps much to keep them on the straight track. Later they may drop it when they have become accustomed to these. In Eng. - Latin work, let them work with patterns again. Only sometime later mention the relative time rule.

Teacher's Manual

40. Give them the translations for all forms of <u>ire</u> listed in the vocabulary. Minimize the importance of the new word order—it will actually cause no trouble.

41. Put on board five sample infinitives—then add -<u>t</u> to all—isn't it easy! Tell them that you are sorry you cannot give a standard translation for this subjunctive. But it is easy if they will follow instructions. 1. Most subjunctives translate just the same as indicatives (for we must confess that the <u>amat</u>, <u>amabant</u>, etc. that we have been using are really called indicatives. Now we need the name to keep them apart from subjunctives). 2. Yet, some are translated in special ways: THE ONLY EASY PRACTICAL WAY IS TO LEARN PATTERNS FOR EACH SPECIAL WAY AS IT COMES UP—there will not be a lot, and not much trouble. Then go over the examples for them. Comment that example 1. uses <u>might</u>, while type 2. does not. How can we tell them apart? In Latin-English it is no problem; use what fits best. Do not tell them the grammatical distinction of adverbial and substantive purpose clauses. Eng.-Lat. sentences are easy enough that there will be no trouble. Then at once (even if first part of lesson has not been done) go through the <u>Exerceamus</u> with books open. It will be advisable to stress frequently in future periods for the next few weeks that most subjunctives translate as indicatives—just a few do not—and add up the few thus far that do not (for some time, only purpose and "horticultural").

42. Dative of pronouns will need little stress. It is easy, and most attention should go to the subjunctive, still, less attention to the 9 adjectives. Suggest memorizing the list in the order given, but do not enforce.

43. On the tense of subjunctive in <u>cum</u> clauses—the distinction between impf. and plu-perf. can be told <u>by the general sense</u>. Do not explain that "plu-perf. means completed action relative to time of main verb, etc." Stress that <u>CUM</u> always means BECAUSE or ALTHOUGH in the Subjunctive. For WHEN, WHILE and AFTER, it varies and the distinction will be learned later. Stress the usefulness of WHILE as tentative translation when they do not know at once which meaning to choose. Lastly, the reason for comment on Anthony is that it was infatuation, not love. The "fatness" of Cleopatra is only relative to today's "ideals".

45. Put on board a pluperfect indicative passive, e.g., amatus erat. Compare to <u>amatus esset</u>. On result clauses, do not give the distinction of substantive and adverbial. But stress, lightly, that we can often tell result from purpose by inserting "so that as a result". Or: Purpose tells what one <u>wants</u>; result tells what actually comes.

46. Put up set of samples on board, make comparisons—but then insist the easiest way to learn is to memorize a set of third singular actives—only five words! On when to use present, as against imperfect subjunctive, patience will be needed—in the Eng.-Lat. sentences if they give the wrong one, just say: "We ought to change the <u>videant</u> to <u>viderent</u> to match the first verb <u>misit</u>. If we had <u>mittit</u>, then <u>videant</u> would be right, etc. If this is done patiently and mechanically, they will develop the right habits without much difficulty. A later lesson will take it up more formally.

Teacher's Manual

47. We now begin to introduce 1st and 2nd person forms. *Here we must be satisfied with a rather wide gap between active and passive mastery.* It will close only slowly, and not entirely in the first year. Place chief stress on translating correctly from Latin to English. Explain that less will be demanded of them in *making* forms (Eng.-Latin) than in *understanding* Latin-Eng. But something needs to be demanded—cf. the sample tests. However, deductions will mount in the second section of the tests for a while. If no more than about a third of a normal class loses more than 10% on the second part, results are satisfactory. But it is surprising how readily they will learn to translate Lat.-Eng. passages. Notice that to translate a 1st or 2nd person form *in context* is more normal and less difficult, than to handle an isolated form in the exams.

50. About the "permission of the 5 pigs"—it is because they say "Oui Oui" (We, We).

51. Not much active mastery can be required for a while on the present indicatives. In presenting, put on board the whole set of forms, draw lines for stick on middle four forms of each set, with line between the vowel and the s, t, mus, tis. Then observe: 1. Each column has six forms—the only irregularities are on the top and bottom forms. The middle four forms are perfectly regular on the old stick. 2. As for the bottom forms, the 3rd plural, some are odd—but — we learned them long ago. 3. So, net result—only really troublesome thing to learn is the first singulars (and that is not so much). A practical way is to memorize one of each of the five across the top. Repeat this same summation on next day also.

53. In presenting the future forms, the same process as given for lesson 51 may be used—point out that it is the same process. Place little stress on imperative.

54. Stress that these verbs are thoroughly irregular only in present indicative—other forms are normal, at least when we get them going. Put up synopsis of forms on board. This lesson is intended for a bit of relief from large blocks of new forms—point out that fact to class.

55. Stress how simple it is to recognize, and even to make forms. Perfect must be considered separately. Present and future indicative: middle four forms use stick—third plural learned long ago—need to memorize only 1st singular. ALL OTHER FORMS, IND. AND SUBJ., USE the m, s, t, mus, tis, nt stick! Not so much as it seemed! Now, or somewhere about this time, is a good time to help a bit to distinguish various uses of that. Put up, and compare, the following four sentences (add Latin translations): 1. He says THAT Caesar is coming. 2. Mary is the girl THAT Marcus loves. 3. He is so evil THAT no one loves him. 4. He came THAT (or: so that, in order that) he might see Caesar.—But one must not expect complete mastery, not even complete passive mastery of isolated sentences containing THAT at this time—sufficient that they can handle the matter given in the text.

56. Follow same style of treatment as in lesson 54.

57. This lesson is intended for a still larger relief—*it merely applies a bit of information we already have.* Put on board: paratus est, parati sumus, and show that we merely add the forms learned in lesson 56 here. Similarly for other

Teacher's Manual

perfects. As to use of perfect subjunctive, recall that most subjunctives translate like indicatives—exceptions thus far are purpose clauses and hortatory subjunctive—but the perfect seldom is used in the latter two, hence almost always translates like the indicative.

58. Stress that the new forms will be less extensive than the active forms were—for there we had to deal with the perfects, along with the present, imperfect, and future. Here we only have the latter three. Less should be demanded in exams and recitation on 1st and 2nd passive forms than in active— for they are much less common. Give little stress to num.

60. Give little stress to <u>aliquid</u> and <u>-que</u>. In regard to the latter, you can use one of the more famous examples: Senatus <u>Populusque</u> Romanus (SPQR).

61. If desired, a form of presentation like that used in lesson 51 can be used (if so, point out that realtion). Put on board the whole set of forms, draw lines for stick on middle four forms of each set (<u>ris</u>, <u>tur</u>, <u>mur</u>, <u>mini</u>). Then observe: Third plurals are a bit odd in some tables—but we learned them before. We must learn the 1st sg. across the top, as we did in lesson 51—and, in addition, the two ringed forms, <u>poneris</u> and <u>caperis</u>. Then write summary on the board: 1. The middle four go on stick. 2. Third pl. learned previously. 3. Learn 1st sg. across the board—and add the exception to #1 (write it now after #1)—except <u>poneris</u> and <u>caperis</u>. No stress on the indefinite pronouns and adj. now. Some like to say: After <u>si</u>, <u>nisi</u>, <u>ne</u>, <u>num</u>, and <u>an</u>: <u>aliquis</u> loses the "ali" (which is right for most forms).

Latin by the Natural Method

62. If desired, may present these forms as in lesson 61. If so, again, the third plurals were learned before—the middle four fit the stick perfectly, except for two ringed forms (paraberis, habeberis)—and must memorize 1st sing. across the top. On vocatives, little stress, but urge them to learn the sample sentence containing all.

63. In the review, stress: It is much like that for all actives. The perfect must be considered separately (as it is easier than active). Present and future indicative—middle four forms use the stick (except: poneris, caperis, paraberis) otherwise, need only to memorize 1st singular. All other forms, indicative and subjunctive behave well on the stick.

64. One could also present the endings of perf. sub. by using the stick. Then add that fut. perf. ind. is the same except for the 1st sg. Place no stress on passive imperatives, except to give a few more examples of deponents.

65. Put up the Hoc est faciendum mihi. Draw lines to show matching of English. Then give also: I must do it. Give a few additional examples. Then present the Veniendum est mihi. It will cause no trouble. Immediately take the Exerceamus of this lesson, even if they have not prepared it in advance. Place little stress on objective of extent (note that per also can be used; we have used it). Nor on mille.

66. Stress that there is nothing new in the sequence rules—just making exact what we have been using. Speak of it as matching subjunctives with the main verb. Stress that we depend on SENSE to pick between impf. & pl. pf. or pres. & pf. Do not mention "action complete or incomplete relative to main verb" etc. No stress on labels.

Teacher's Manual

67. On the purpose: could also tell them to translate ad by for, and then make <u>videndum</u> mean "seeing". Some find this easier. This helps with <u>causa</u> and <u>gratis</u>. ("for the sake of seeing"). And the -<u>ing</u> translation works with all -<u>ndus</u> forms except the obligation use! Place a little stress on dative of possession.

68. For the gerunds, we must use the -<u>ing</u> translations. Point out then that all but the obligation use can have the -<u>ing</u> translations. Place a little stress on double dative.

69. For the fut. inf. in Ind. disc.—give a pair of patterns, to add to previous examples, and urge them again to work by examples, not by the relative time method: Dicit Caesarem venturum esse: He says that C will come. Dixit Caesarem venturum esse: He said that C would come. A little stress on double objective.

71. Comparatives will be no problem, should not be stressed too much. Go over list of irregulars and note which ones they have not yet had. Abl. of comparison: Is really a from ablative. Draw two men on board, one taller than other, with an arrow pointing from level of lower head to level of top head: Joseph is taller from (the level of) Pharao. But put little stress on it.

72. Little stress on adverbs. But go over irregular list, point out which are new to them. Still less stress on 4th decl. neut. and on <u>domus</u> and <u>iste</u>.

73. On Real Conditions, do not stress labels. Even imitation of models is not much needed here, just let them

translate naturally. Only warning needed is that English uses present for future in _if_ part of future reals.

75. Point out that some _if_ sentences in English have "special" forms of the verb compare to examples in lesson 73, and note the "_would_". Stress: sentences that have would in the conclusion need subjunctive in Latin. For tenses: imitate the models. Spend very little time on _malle_.

76. Demonstrate each example in the steps given (may, if preferred, insert the English preposition in the third step). Add a few examples of your own.

77. Point out that we have been using some impersonal verbs for some time. Little stress is needed, particularly on those that are not always impersonal—further reading next year will take care of them. Note that we have already on several occasions used from or because of to translate abl. without prep. Do not bother with distinctions of when to use or omit Latin preps. with these ablatives.

78. The three English translations to cover all uses of fut. pass. etc, are: 1. TO BE plus the English passive participle. 2. English Infinitive. 3. English gerund (_ing_) Note also that -_ing_ can be used for all but the obligation (as mentioned earlier). A short form of these rules for conditions would be: All reals are indicative, with obvious tenses; all ideals are subjunctive with tenses 1 notch off. Recall also that ideals have "wooden" conclusions in English. In vocabulary—note that _nimis_ (and _nimius_) in Late Latin need not mean "_too_ much"—may mean merely "very much".

Teacher's Manual

79. Little stress on locative. But note that all three major place relations have no preposition (ordinarily) with names of towns etc. (i.e., going to, coming from, staying in—which are: objective, abl., and locative, or abl. where there is no locative).

80 - 81. Little stress on new matters in these lessons—all will be repeated next year.

IV. Set of examinations and sample oral questions

Function of exams: The examinations are not solely to give information on achievement of students—more reliable and abundant information comes from daily calls. Exams do, of course, supplement that information. But the exams serve also to stimulate precision. Without them students could take undue advantage of the fact that perfect active control is not demanded so soon as in other methods. *The exams are carefully designed to call for just the right amount of active control.* This will appear chiefly in the second part of the exams. An average student ordinarily should not lose more than 10 percent on that second part (except during that part of the year when a large number of new forms—1st and 2nd person—are being presented). If too many lose too much in the second part, future tests should again check on the same items. Most of the exam, however, is given to vocabulary, for that is the most essential thing, as studies have shown. Note: On the day before the first exam, put up on board samples of the type of question to be used, with sample answers. The number of each exam indicates the lesson after which it could be used. To save space, items are not numbered below. Except for the first

Latin by the Natural Method

exam, there are 20 vocabulary items, and 10 items on forms and structures. In the vocabulary items (except for the first exam) the student is to complete the vocabulary listing of each item, e.g., if any part of a verb is given, student gives other parts and meaning. If meaning is given, student gives parts that are known by that time. Similarly for nouns. In part II, student is always to translate (if some parts of an item are underlined, only those parts are to be translated). An asterisk separates items of parts I and II.

Exams for First Year

4. (In this first exam only, have them simply translate all forms and combinations), remanserunt, invenit, est, quando, iam, iecit, viderunt, quod, he gave, they had, he saw, they reigned, when, Maria amavit virum, they gave money, before the city, with the lamb, fuit in urbe, cecidit in aquam. (last 6 items count 8 points, others 4 each).

8, Fecerunt, sunt, fere, creavit, quia, ceperunt, civis, scivit, res, multus, they willed (wished), now, always, he conquered, field, new, power, senate, they sent, he wrote." Maria amavit the king, Vidit the danger, Marcus fuit in the senate. Pons cecidit into the water. Regina dedit the money. Plebs voluit power. Roma fuit magna in planning. Primis diebus Roma bellum habuit. Galli venerunt exercitibus magnis. Romani vicerunt Gallon magna potentate.

12. Posse, servavit, timet, regnavit, scire, videre, velle, mare, auxilium, pones., ask, send, prepare, remain, come, conquer, name, father, hand, receive.* Marcus saw the good lamb. Marcus saw a good sailor. Marcus saw a bad pig. Marcus came with the good kings. Marcus came with a

Teacher's Manual

large army. Marcus came with a bad pig. Bellum fuit great. Urbs fuit large. Maria fuit good. Romani vicerunt fortitudine magna.

16. De, accepit, non iam, iter, miles, dedit, visas, ease, frigidus, audire, have, send, put (place), through, love (verb), do, river, fear, mountain, capture. * He had asked. He was asked. They were prepared. She has been seen. Marcus vidit brave soldiers. Marcus habuit a good name. Navis fuit in the fierce sea. Bellum fuit sharp, Primis diebus Romani fuerunt magni consiliis. (The last item counts double).

20. Pro, saepe, debere, vicit, responsum, licet, frumentum, sine, aedificavit, depositus, destroy, all, apart, bravely, call, depart, order (verb), place (noun), easy, speech. *The father of Marcus, legates of the Romans, he had come, she has been seen, he saw those men, that woman is here, he came with a brave sailor, agno audito porci dixerunt oink, Maria visa Marcus dixit O! After the Romans had been conquered Hannibal was glad.

24. Modus, verus, afuit, misericordia, consuetudo, movit, praesertim, proponere, ira, tenere. time, they were (do not use fuerunt), while, kill, punish, better, doubt (noun), hope (verb), place (verb), hear. *He had seen, he had been seen, she had been killed, Marcus discessit cum this man, Columbus habuit those ships, they are seizing, she loves, Caesare interfecto. Brutus discessit, Caesar misericordia motus est, because he had seen the lamb. Marcus was angry (do not use quia).

28. Fregit, ibi. divisit, accidit, evadere, ductus, pauci, audax, discere, vinculum, flee, however, seize (not capere),

Latin by the Natural Method

once upon a time, life. although, difficult, greater, four, three. *Marcus vidit the same man, Maria venit cum her, viderunt them in foro, viri venerunt who Mariam amaverunt, vir whom Maria amat est Marcus, she is placing, he has been placed, auditus erat, Caesar himself came, I saw Caesar himself.

32. Egit, invidia aut, conari. praevidit, redire, insuper, locutus eat, dimittere. mori, such, follow, expect, gate. accuse. meanwhile, not yet, town, ask, think. *To be loved, he gives money to the soldiers, he comes to the city, I want to see, he attempted, he is being captured, he is capturing, locuta est, audiuntur, auditi sunt.

36. (Or 35.) If after 35, use the words in parentheses in the first section instead of those outside parentheses. Second section the same for either lesson 35 or 36). Legere, equus, profectus est, monuit, reverti, ostendere, novit, fieri (coniuratio), propter (gladius), initium (quare), be born, book, for a long time, famous, answer (verb), foot, live. read (order-noun), virtue (writer), proud (month).* They were following, he was warning, he was being heard, whose, of the same man, of those men, volebat, Maria veniente Marcus laetus erat, Mariam venientem Marcus vidit, Maria videns Marcum exclamavit.

40. Forsan, socius, alibi, narravft, hostis, consultus, affecit, aggredi, profanare, prison, prove, cause, arrest, mystery, grief, horse, go, please, my. * Tenebunt, ponetur, he will be loved, they will hear, whom did he see? to have seen, a quibus haec accepit? Catalina dicit se venisse in senatum., Marcus dixit se Mariam amare. Mary said that she had seen Marcus (do not use quod construction).

Teacher's Manual

44. Requiescere, privare, cum (not preposition), quotidie, ignovit, pepulit, similis, nolle, proximus, relictus, teach, light, if, old, beautiful, give back, lest, short, permit, night. *<u>Cui</u>, he gave money <u>to one man</u>, <u>cum vidisset</u> agnum, dixit; <u>cum Mariam amaret</u> agnum odit. agnus venit ut audiret magistrum, dixit se amare scholam, he sent men <u>to find</u> Brutus, he thinks <u>that Caesar is</u> good, <u>huic</u> viro, dedit pecuniam <u>ei</u>.

48. Deinde, abscondere, interrogatus, num, comedit, tam, sentire, protulit, nescivit, fefellit, believe, body, command (not <u>iubere</u>), voice, wood, sign, so great, obey, mind, kind, race. * Translate subjunctives same as indicatives, but mark "S": Vobis, paravisses, amavissemus, amarem, audiat, audiet, let him come, let us hear, he spoke so loud <u>that</u> all heard.

52. Nisi, finire, clausit, civitas, confidere, ruptus, mutavit, egressus est, iterum, fames, why, bring, ancestors, never, or, terrify, rich, master, appear, behold. *Translate and mark subjunctives as "S": Amo, ponitis, amaveramus. audivisti, ponatis. I come, you (sing.) have, to me, we have seen, he comes <u>that he may find Mary</u>.

59. Tollere, voluntas, apparuit, gens, pepercit, dormivit, circumstare, unde, prodesse, vendidit, touch, worship, bread, fill, delay, certainly, draw, drag, be present, pour. word. *Translate and mark subjunctives "S" but translate as indicatives): Amabo, pones, ponas, ponis, sum, via, loquaris, coner, amate,

63. Antea, constituit, emit, tum, calix, abstulit, adducere, oblitus est. praecepit, pollicitus est, cross, govern, business, turn, favor, grace, nevertheless, put in charge of, wisdom,

hand over, mouth. *(Translate the subjunctive as indicative but mark "S"): Amabor, amabar, audiris, audiaris, of anyone, he will hear, may he hear, we are being killed, he is loved, do you see <u>someone</u>?

66. Abiit, reperire, at, mille, flevit, consequi, mandavit, peccare, accessit, nocuit, lose, safety, grieve, secretly, suffer, think, carry, smallest, even if, authority. *(Translate the following, but translate the subjunctive as indicative but mark "S"): He will have loved, they have come, I shall love, amaverim, amavero, frumentum portandum est nobis, discedendum est mihi, we must see Caesar, a thousand soldiers, two thousand soldiers.

70. Oculus, exercuit, appropinquavit, durus, cupere, os, cernere, tribuit, iuvit, mos, except, rule, age, be strong, bless, best, punishment, heavy, run, until. *Equites venerunt <u>auxilio nobis</u>, <u>Marco equus bonus est</u>, misit milites <u>ad Catilinam capiendum</u>, <u>frumenti emendi causa venimus</u>, <u>Caesar venturus erat</u>, <u>Caesarem equum rogat</u>, <u>dixit Hebraeos discessuros esse</u>, <u>ad dormiendum</u> discessit, currendo evaserunt, <u>amor regendi</u> duxit eum in periculum.

74. Joseph went out <u>to weep</u> (do not use subj. cl.), the king has wisdom (do not use <u>habere</u>), Mary has a love <u>of speaking</u>, he said <u>that the brothers would carry grain</u> (no <u>quod</u> clause), Catalina dicitur Ciceronem interfecturus esse, <u>flendo</u> Iosephus ostendit dolorem suum, these pigs are much heavier than those pigs, Cicero spoke <u>much better</u>, si ille sapientiam habet somnium interpretari poterit, (make this into a conditional sentence): Forsan fames in Aegypto non est. Forsan frumentum venditur ibi.

Teacher's Manual

<u>Latin I Final</u> Vocabulary: Solvit, percutere, conspexit, quoque, praebere, negatus, statutus, auxit, persuade, fresh, pray, hinder, join, be lacking, wound. *Translate: We must buy grain (use fut. pass. part.): he was sent to Egypt <u>to help his brothers</u>, the lamb has many friends (do not use habere), he showed his courage by <u>fighting well</u>, Marcus is <u>good</u> Crassus is <u>better</u> my friends are <u>best</u>, Crassus said that Caesar would not depart (do not use <u>quod</u>), he learned the art <u>of fighting</u>, Crassus was at Rome <u>when I was</u> at Athens (use <u>cum</u>), forsan Gilgamesh viderit me Forsan ille interficiet me (convert to cond. sentence): Iosephus non est vir malus. Iosephus fratres non punit (convert to cond. sentence), he showed his goodness <u>in helping his brother</u>, <u>discendendum</u> est antequam Catilina nos videat, the senate had the custom <u>of sending legates</u>, <u>we must work</u> (use fut. pass. part. of <u>laborare</u>), <u>fratrum probandorum causa</u> haec fecit.

Exams for Second Year:
4. quando, vidit, fecit, fere, civis, timuit, scire, posuit, mare, flumen, homo, loqui, quamquam, duxit, accidit, horse, return, four, ask, die, often, without, conquer, hear, destroy, power, be able, truth, order (verb), kill. * He fell <u>into the river</u>. He conquered them with great power. They have been killed. We saw <u>many brave sailors</u>. The city was <u>large and fierce</u>. <u>His auditis,</u> milites discesserunt. <u>After the citizens had been killed</u>, the king was glad (not <u>postquam</u> or <u>cum</u>). He saw <u>these same seas</u>. The Romans were <u>good in plans</u>. <u>Because Marcus' father had not been heard</u>, Marcus was angry (not <u>cum</u>, <u>quia</u> or <u>quod</u>).

8. similis, noluit, imperare, obedivit, claudere, nisi, egredi, foedus, sanguis, oblivisci, teach, night, believe, voice,

worst, fill, will (noun) kill, nevertheless, only. *Vir whom Maria amat est Marcus. Certain men saw Caesar himself. He is being heard. He said that Marcus was being killed (do not use quod clause). While Caesar was shouting, they fought bravely (use a participle as part of structure). He is said to have killed many men. Imperavit ludaeis that they fight bravely. Because he had asked the Lord night did not come (use cum). His face was so glorious that they feared to look. He will be captured.

12. servire, tenebrae, via, sedit, vadere, solere, quicumque, crescere, inquit, earnere, lose, go out, be strong, 1000, think, heart, guard, how, enter, begin. *Quem cum vidisset exclamavit. He came to hear the teacher (use subj.). He said that he found water (not quod). He spoke so loudly that all heard. Let us fight bravely. We are brave men. You (sg.) are speaking (not dicere). Follow me! (plural). If you see any ship, call me. Venias. Qui venerunt ad regem.

16. abscindere, reperuit, defecit, metus, vultus, scidit, diligere, eruit, sinere, praeda, bless, desire, walk, harm(verb), wonder at, whoever, beware, displease, understand, bring to. *The priest Heli must die (use gerundive). They traveled forty years. He was sent to find the king (gerundive). Regi sunt amici. Saluti vobis veni. The king will be obeyed. By coming he obeyed the king. He thought that, the king would not see him (not quod). He is said to be about to come. He taught the king wisdom.

20. animadvertere, ubicumque, consequi, simul, iuvit, quoniam, exaudivit, adicere, mandavit, ieiunare, deny, rush, secretly, rule, knee, be glad, side, scorn, punishment. flock. *Dicit Marcum esse better. Dicit eum esse better than Paul

Teacher's Manual

(no quam). They fought much more bravely. If he had known the truth he would not have come. By killing the man, he did wrong. If it should rain, I would not come. Scripsit multa de pueris docendis. Marcus said that Mary would come (inf. constr.) If I were king, I would not act thus. He is bravest of all.

24. mirari, adhibuit, refert, avertere. silva, cornu, lavare, vestigium. debilis, obsecrare, fulfill, prohibit, except, according to, at least, refuse, not even, add, take care of, wise. *He saw a man braver than Caesar. If they had not done evil, they would have been spared. He ran most swiftly. Parcendum est mihi. He wrote a book about capturing cities. Saul dixit eum regnaturum esse. The means of seeking peace are known. When I was at Rome you were at Athens. Rogavit Caesar for money. Viro in locum periculosum ponendo peccavit.

30. peperit, mundare, succendit, alere, pariter, lugere, apud, mentitus, impetrare, deprecari, past, tempt, spot, knowledge. cruel, authority, hinder, be silent, custom, prayer. *Venientibus hostibus, Iudaei non timuerunt. Visis quos timebant exercitibus, fortiter pugnaverunt. Ingressa in palatium, Esther territa est. Virum indutum sacco viderunt (on previous 4 items, give first literal, then expanded translation. On next 3 items, paraphrase in Latin). Pugnantibus fortiter rex dona dedit. Opera laborantium laudavit dux. Recensentes in bibliotheca rex vidit. (On next 3 items translate with participle if possible). He hated those who were following him. To him who conquers Goliath, he gives gifts. Having tried this, the man left.

35. arbitratus, supplicium, finxit, gemere, frustra, ambito, optare, cecinit, gradatim, mundare, quickly, bring about, encourage, hope, give thanks. attack (noun), joy, lion, witness. here. *(On first three items, paraphrase in Latin, then translate): <u>Credentibus</u> praemia debit. <u>Venientium</u> gladios spectat. <u>Ingredientes</u> in urbem <u>occidet</u> rex. (On next 4 items, give first literal translation, then free). <u>Haec locutus dux discessit</u>. <u>Milites interfectos</u> spectavit. <u>Veniente quem timebant exercitu fugerunt</u>. <u>Viso periculo</u> mortuus est. (On next 3 items, translate, using part. or abl. abs.) <u>Those who were coming were happy</u>. The hearts <u>of those who were fighting were brave</u>. <u>After he had pursued them</u> three hours, he stopped.

40. exorare, gaudere, dilectio, exercere, largiri. pondus, labi, fiducia. convenire, proles, increase, make joyful, fatherland, wound (noun), reverence (verb), vice, pray, establish, daily (adj.) cease.* <u>Qui haec viderunt</u> timebant. <u>Quibus rex praemia dedit</u>. <u>Viso somnio</u> territus est rex. <u>Veniente duce</u>, milites laboraverunt. <u>Quod mititibus non placuit</u>. <u>Qui Caesarem sequebantur servati sunt</u>. <u>A quibus Caesar servatus est</u>. <u>Multa locutus,</u> Cato plura dixit. <u>We who sin</u> should pray much. <u>And he came into the city</u> (use relative if possible on this last item).

44. item, agnovit, scelestus, opus est, denique, cessit. sprevit, testari, praestare, ops, heavenly, mike holy, abundance, foolish, safe, be awake, peaceful, admonish, equal, eat. *<u>Qui peccamus</u> mali sumus. <u>Multi homines num vivant difficile est scire</u>. <u>Quibus militibus gladios dedit etiam pecuniam dabit</u>. <u>Placendum est divinis oculis</u> habitu corporis. <u>Venientibus</u> ad orationem concordis debet esse. <u>Eos secutus</u> tres horas dux reversus est. Judas <u>percussis</u>

Teacher's Manual

multis hostibus laetus erat. The prayer <u>of those who love God</u> is good (transl. in one word). <u>Having learned the truth</u>, he did not accept it (use participle). <u>When the soldiers were captured</u> the general was glad.

48. deliquit, praestare, testari, yenta, secundum quad, patuit, scilicet, reprobare. tectum. necare, redeem, scarcely, criticize, refresh, hesitate, to watch, equal, mindful of, imitate, kind *<u>Qui hoc fecerunt</u> viri mali erant. <u>Haec locutus dux discessit. Hi plus in equitibus</u>, <u>ills in militibus confidunt</u>. <u>Orantium</u> vita bona debet ease. <u>Having captured Catiline</u> Cicero was safe. <u>We must obey the Lord</u> (use gerundive or fut. pass. part.). <u>Facienti quod potest</u> Dominus non negat gratiam. They killed <u>those who were coming</u> (participle). <u>You who do these things</u> are evil men. <u>Vidi hos homines quod</u> fortes erant.

SAMPLE ORAL QUESTIONS: Tell the students to look away from the book in answering *when they can*—when they can't, use the book for whatever help it is. Note that -ne is not required in oral Latin. Urge students to answer in complete sentences wherever possible, even though answer would be clear in a few words—better practice. In framing questions, try to work in a moderate number of examples of new forms and structures, and also, to reuse some previously introduced items. Care must be taken, however, not to make it too difficult, nor to demand too much active mastery in this way.

1. (Supply: Quis, quid, ubi, utique on the blackboard). Quis habuit parvum agnum? Quid habuit Maria? Fuit agnus albus? Quis venit in scholam? Quis venit cum Maria? Quis vidit agnum in schola? Quid dixit agnus? Quiz fuit in schola cum Maria? Ubi hit Maria? Ubi fuit agnus? Quiz fuit in

schola cum Maria at agno? Quis fuit albus? Dixit Marcus baa? Quis dixit baa? Fuit Columbus regina? Quid non habuit Columbus? Quis venit ad babeLiam. Quid dixit Columbus Isabella. (don't worry about dative—they will follow from word order—and so later on can get away with a few things similarly)? Fuit mundus planus ? Fuit Columbus rotundus? Fuit Isabella rotunda? Quid dedit Isabella? Quid invenit Columbus? Fuit America parva.

15. (Note: Whenever important new structures have been introduced recently, it is good to work a few examples into the questions or answer): Quis est victus ad flumen Trebiam? Quis vicit ad hoc flumen? Quo anno fecit Hannibal aliam victoriam? Quis victus est proximo anno? A quo victus est? Quid dixit Flaminius de Hannibal.? Dixitne Flaminius veritatem? Quare dixit Flaminius hoc ? Timuitne Hannibal nivem? Quare timuit Roma? Quid fecit Hannibal? A quo factae aunt insidiae? Ubi fuit Flaminius et exercitus Romans? Ubi posit sunt milites Punici? Quis fuit ante exercitum Romanum? Potuerunt Romani milites videre Punicos? Quare non potuerunt videre Punicos ? Ubi fuerunt nebulae? Quis victus est at Lacum Trasimenum? Quis vicit ad Lacum Trasimenum?

41. (Partial list only). Quis pugnavit contra Caesarem in belle civili? Quomodo dedit Caesar auxilium Ciceroni quando in exsilio erat? Quo tempore reversus est Cicero Romam? Quis rogavit ut Cicero reverteretur? Reversus est Cicero ut pugnaret pro Pompeio? Venerat Cicero ut contra Caesarem pugnaret? Quare venit Cicero in castra Pompei? Pugnavit Cicero fortiter in hoc belle? Quare fugit Pompeius? In quam terram fugit ut servaretur? Vixit Pompeius in Aegypto multos annos? Bello finito, quomodo

Teacher's Manual

punivit Caesar Ciceronem? Vocavit Caesar Ciceronem ut puniret eum?

54. (Let those who answer do so in the first person, speaking as Abraham, and do in like manner in several following lessons). Qui es tu? Quid est nomen tuum? Habuisti hoc nomen semper? Qui dedit tibi nomen novum? Quo tempore natus es? Ex qua terra venisti? Ex qua civitate? In qua parte Babyloniae est Ur? Habes multos deos? Quid de aliis hominibus in Ur, habentne multos deos? Colit pater tuus multos deos? Quid de fratre tuo? Estne frater tuus adhuc in hac vita? Quo tempore venisti in Haran? Colunt homines in Haran unum Deum verum? Quid significat hoc verbum "Sin"? Vidisti Deum tuum? Audivisti eum? Ubi eras quando apparuit tibi? Quid dixit Deus tibi? Quis venit ex Haran tecum? Habuisti multos annos cum venires ex Haran? Quis est uxor tua? In quam terram descendisti ex Haran? Quare non remansisti in illa terra? In quam terram venisti ex Chanaan? Remansisti per longum tempus in Aegypto? Habesne multas possessiones? Habetne Lot etiam multas? Habitat Lot adhuc tecum? Quare non? Ubi est Lot nunc? Suntne homines in Sodomia magni virtute? Punist Deus tuna Sodoma? Rogavisti Deum tuum pro his hominibus? Suntne homines in Sodomis deleti? Qui duxit Lot ex Sodomis? Ubi est uxor Lot nunc? Quid accidit ei? Quare accidit hoc? Quomodo destruxit Deus Sodoma? Destruxit Deus etiam alias civitates eodem tempore? Ubi nunc est locus harum civitatum?

Latin by the Natural Method

SUGGESTIONS FOR TEACHING SECOND YEAR
GENERAL NOTIONS

1. The basic theory and practice remain the same as first year, but now we gradually demand more active mastery than last year. At the end of the year (see below) we will spend about a month on intense work for active mastery, but even earlier in the year we gradually increase demands.

2. Insist on precise and exact translation, even when a loose translation gives the sense: it is important to cultivate habits of accuracy. The need will become more apparent in second semester.

3. When a student stumbles on a sentence, insist particularly that he (and others who had trouble) go over that line even more than the usual half dozen times. When time permits, it is good for the teacher to read such sentences over 6 times in class. When a piano student stumbles, he does not merely go on—if he does, he does not develop—but he repeats the passage many times. The case is similar in Latin. If a student merely gets the intellectual solution to a difficulty, he has done the hard part—and a needed part—but has lost the most efficient part of the practice if he does not go over that spot many times. He failed because he did not have automatic habits of the type needed for that pattern. The number of patterns is great, but not infinite—and there is much overlap. So if he "makes friends" with each difficulty as it comes, he will find eventually that he seldom has cause to stumble. Before giving the student the answer, insist that he pick out subject, verb, and object, in that order, and translate them in

Teacher's Manual

that order, leaving all else out. If this is done, he will almost always get the translation without other help.

4. Since students have become very rusty during the summer, the difficulty of the matter in the first 4 lessons is lower than that at the end of 1st year. Similarly, they will need review. This is provided for in the first 12 lessons, which review lessons 1-64 of first year. Lsssons 13-24 cover the matter of lessons 65-81 of first year. This provides for flexibility: a teacher can leave off at any point after lesson 64 of 1st year. Matter covered in first year beyond lesson 64 will be treated as review in second year: matter not covered can be learned for the first time in lessons 13-24 of second year.

5. In general, during the Old Testament lessons (1-35) each lesson can be done in two or at most three periods. In the first half of the allotted time, cover the story matter. In the second half, cover the remainder of the lesson. Thus the Old Testament matter (35 lessons) should be finished by about the end of the first semester. When lesson 39 is reached, one day per week should be devoted to the English to Latin matter in back (pp.136-55), devoting one period to each unit, following the procedure for English- Latin given above, [revise page] p,12. After lesson 48 is completed, every day should he given to this English - Latin until it is completed. It is hoped that this can all be finished by about one month before the end of the school year. The last month can then be spent on grammatical sharpening. For this, go back to lesson 39, retranslate all of St. Cyprian, but also ask students to identify and classify various bits of grammar. In this way we imitate the ideal situation found in some natives: they first learn to handle their language by

Latin by the Natural Method

automatic habits—then, later, they (may) go to school, and receive intensive grammar work. This is beneficial if done after automatic habits are solidly grounded: harmful if done sooner (for if done too soon, the student will begin to handle the language by grammar analysis instead of by habits, which would be unfortunate).

6. Throughout the year, it is extremely important to have a minimum and a volunteer period for translation of stories and other connected matter, In the minimum section, call on students by name, and have them read the Latin before translating. Announce that all must translate correctly in the minimum section for even a C grade (with the possible exception of a specially difficult spot). All who hope for an A or B must also be ready for the volunteer period. There, accept volunteers only; do not have them read the Latin aloud before translating. Raise the minumum assignment gradually throughout the year (in a 50 minute period, about 30...minutes should be given to the minimum section). The volunteer section will often cover twice again as much as the minimum period. But watch lest some students skip either the minimum (if teacher calls on best students only for the volunteer period) or the early part of the volunteer section, to give the impression that they have prepared more than they really have done: only consistent offering to translate proves they have done it all.

SPECIFIC SUGGESTIONS

Lessons 1-2. Since students are rusty begin very slowly. All through the year, cover all stories both by exact translation and by oral questions. But in the first two lessons, cover stories by translation twice: once with books open, once with books, closed.

Teacher's Manual

7. It is time to refresh the technique of word order practice from last year. Explain the method again, and use the following sentences for practice: Pompeium, amicum nostrum, in via Caesar vidit. Caesarem cum porco venientem vidit Brutus. Marcum qui porcum habuit, non amavit magister. Hunc hominem, quem multi oderant, non odit mater eius. Linguam Latinam. cum facila sit, in schola celeriter discunt multi. Venerunt in terram nostram. quam vehementer amamus, duo exploratores. In hoc deserto, quia aquam non habebant, contra Moysen murmuraverunt Israelitae. Portaverunt per desertum, ubi per annos multos fuerunt, Iudaei corpus Iosephi. Populo clamanti locutus est multa verba Moyses. Amicis meis, quos per multos annos amavi, multa dona dedit Paulus. Hos viros, postquam in urbem ingressi sunt, Sulla interfecit. Ex hac urbe egressi sunt, et in castra nostra venerunt, multi milites.

8. Give word order practice with the following sentences having 2 sidetracks each. Explain that the last sidetrack (ST) to open must be the first to close. Formula: Main opens, ST1 opens, ST2 opens, ST3 opens, ST3 closes, ST2 closes, ST1 closes, the Main closes. Ciceronem, qui contra Antonium, quem oderat, orations habuerat, milites Antoni interfecerunt. Hominem hunc, cum multum frumentum vinumque, quae domi habuerat, in castra tulisset, Caesar laudavit. Use 4 steps, as in Scramble of lesson 25 of the 1st year.

9. Word order practice on: Marcus Porcius Cato, cum amicos suos, qui contra Caesarem pugnaverant, laudavisset, sese interfecit. Hominem qui, quamquam multam pecuniam habet, pauperibus auxilium non dat, non debemus honorare.

Latin by the Natural Method

10. Word order practice on: Pompeius, inimicus Caesaris, cum equos, quos hic amisisset, invenisset, eos in castra sua duxit. Ab homine qui, quia non laboravit, non multa didicit, non possums multa rogararet.

11. Word order practice: Ciceroni, qui in bello civili, quia senatum amavit, in castris remansit Pompeii, Caesar ignovit. Quamquam potestatem Mithradatis, qui in provinciam Romanam exercitum duxerat, non fregerat, in urbem reverus est Sulla.

13 - 24. See suggestions in first year section of this manual for lessons 65 - 81.

21. Word order practice: Filium Bethsabee, quia illa rogaverat, regnaturum esse promisit David. Malum filium Absalom, qui contra patrem pugnaverat, pendere ex quercu vidit nuntius. Hunc filium, cum rex David imperavisset, non servatum esse a Ioab dixit nuntius.

22. Word order practice: Se velle, cum rex Solomon rogavisset, cedros caedere scripsit Hiram. Servos suos cedros, qui in Libano erant, caesuros ease promisit rex. Templum magnum ut Domino placeret, se velle facere dixit Salomon.

23. For another way to bring out distinction of indicative and subjunctive with <u>cum</u> temporal in secondary sequence, see lst yr. pattern tape script, 80 B, noting that the indicative is used when there is *no connection* between the two events; they merely *happen to come* at same time.

Teacher's Manual

25 – 28. Insist firmly that each participle (in or out of an absolute) be translated twice: first in the crude basic form, next in one or more good expanded translations. This is to prevent looseness.

36. Rate of speed will drop notably. Watch class psychology: explain that the drop is to be expected, for these are, in all of about the same difficulty as the Scrambles. But stress also the rich gain to be had from much rereading of them. Insist strongly on finding subject, verb, object, and translating them in that order, leaving out all else—but do this only when a student fails to translate otherwise. In the same situation, where needed, insist also on carefully following switching and sidetrack principles.

39. Watch class psychology again on beginning Cyprian. Use the better students to get the first lesson going well, bring in others after a few paragraphs. Oral questions will need to be fewer, quite concrete and simple. But carefully picked questions will go easily and well. It is very helpful too to read the text of St. Cyprian to the class before they try to prepare it: for intelligent reading, with good phrasing and intonation gives much more help than the printed page can. When English - Latin work begins, suggest that they make, on cards or slips, a list of all Latin conjunctions, with meanings, moods, and page on which found, e.g. make one card reading: <u>Quamquam</u>, w. ind., <u>although</u>, p. 138; <u>Ut</u>. w. subj., <u>in order that</u>. p.143. When all conjunctions have been so listed, then sort cards alphabetically, and retype a list; two lists would be good, one English - Latin, one Latin - English. For additional practice, have them translate the same sentences in many ways, especially stress using participles and abl. abs. as substitutes for clauses.

Latin by the Natural Method

47. Again watch class psychology and proceed as in lesson 39.

ADDENDUM
Sources of Collects, etc, pp. 95-103 of 2nd year.

The prayers used are Collects, Secrets, Postcommunions, Orationes super populum from the following days:

1. Ember Saturday of Lent
2. 4th Sunday of Lent
3. August 4th
4. June 11th
5. Wed. after Pentecost
6. February 4th
7. 23rd Sun. after Pentecost
8. Rogation
9. Feb. 2nd
10. Mon. 2nd week of Lent
11. Quinquagesima
12. Ascension
13. July 20th
14. July 10th
15. Dec. 26th
16. Mon. 3rd week of Lent
17. June 10th
18. Dec. 24th
19. Corpus Christi
20. Feb. 6th
21. Aug 17th
22. Christ the King
23. July 31st
24. Dec .17th
25. June 4th
26. 5th Sun. after Pentecost
27. Thurs. 2nd week of Lent
28. 24th Sun. after Pent.
29. Dec. 29th
30. Dec. 21st
31. 5th Sun. after Easter
32. 1st Sun. after Easter
33. June 11th
34. March 25th
35. Mon. 3rd week of Lent
36. August 7th.
37. Fri. 3rd week of Lent
38. Monday of Holy Week
39. November 22nd
40. Passion Sunday
41. Fri. after Ash Wednesday
42. August 31st
43. March 7th
44. Mon. 3rd week in Lent
45. 10th Sun. after Pentecost
46. December 7th
47. May 17th
48. 23rd Sun. after Pentecost
49. December 3rd
50. September 14th
51. Christmas
52. July 19th
53. February 15th
54. July 23rd
55. September 16th
56. January 15th
57. Mon. let week of Lent
58. July 7th
59. September 22nd
60. July 17th
61. Ste. Philip & James
62. 4th week of Lent
63. Monday alter Pentecost
64. Wed. of Passion Week
65. 1st Sun. after Easter
66. June 2nd
67. December 4th
68. Ember Fri. of Lent
69. Thurs. of Passion Week
70. May 26th
71. Sept. 29th
72. Ember Sat. of Lent
73. October 7th
74. Thurs. 2nd week of Lent
75. Sacred Heart
76. 5th Sun. after Epiph.
77. December 27th
78. September 14th
79. November 14th
80. June 11th
81. February 15th
82. 10th Sun. after Pent.
83. Thurs. 4th week of Lent
84. 5th Sun. after Epiph.
85. Holy Name
86. 3rd Sun. after Epiph.
87. Wed. 3rd week of Lent
88. June 6th
89. January 29th
90. November 23rd
91. Friday Passion Week
92. 2nd Sun. after Easter
93. Wed. 2nd week of Lent
94. September 22nd
95. St. Angela
96. Fri. 4tk week of Lent
97. Emb. Sat. of Lent
98. Holy Sat. (old 6th orat.)
99. Christmas
100. Easter

Teacher's Manual

KEY TO ENGLISH TO LATIN
AND
SCRAMBLES OF BOOK I
(Roman Numerals Refer to Lessons)

IX
1. Maria agnum amavit. 2. Maria agnum invenire voluit. 3. Romani Pyrrhum viderunt.

X
1. Romani in periculo erant. 2. Marcus ad urbem venire potuit. 3. Marcus dixit quod Columbus fuit bonus.

XI
1. Columbus magnam veritatem scivit. 2. Isabella multam pecuniam habuit. 3. Roma dives magnos habuit.

XII
1. Quando venit Hannibal? 2. Hamilcar dixit quod Roma mala fuit. 3. Sed Roma pacem voluit.

XIII
1. Marcus vidit milites feroces. 2. Pugna fuit acris. 3. Venit cum viris fortibus.

XIV
1. Exercitus Punicus in Galliam missus est. 2. Multum aurum inventum est. 3. Equites auditi sunt.

Latin by the Natural Method

XV

1. Cincinnatus rogatus est venire. 2. Marcus visus est Mariam amare. 3. Fabula scripta erat. 4. Pecunia missa est.

XVI

1. Hannibal a Romanis victus est. 2 Sed Romanos in multi. pugnis vicerat. 3. Hannibal fuit imperator fortis.

XVII

1. Columbus in mundum novum navigavit. 2. Carthago a frumento interclusa est. 3. Masinissa multum aurum accepit. 4. Multo auro accepto, milites laeti erant. 5. Romanis victis, Hannibal non erat laetus. 6. Frumento accepto, viri imperatorem vocaverunt.

XVIII

1. Pater nautae venerat. 2. Potestas senatus erat magna.
3. Popilius Antiochum discedere iussit. 4. Navis auro capto, imperator non discessit. 5. Antequam nautae Romae venerunt, non erat pugna. 6. Potestas Romae magna fuit.
7. Antiochus rex Seleuciae fuit.

XIX

1. Ubi est ille vir? 2. Maria agnum illum invenire voluit. 3. Viri Romae fortes fuerunt. 4. Cato voluit illos urbem delere. 5. Ille (vir) orationem non amavit. 6. Oratione illa habits, Cato discessit. 7. Magna oratione, urbem delevit.

XX

1. Necesse est feminam invenire. 2. Magna pars militum venit. 3. Sine licentia Romanorum pugnaverunt. 4. Illa (femina) fortis est. 5. Magna pars militum visa est (visi

sunt). 6. Romani magna cum potentate venerunt. 7. Legati Romae iusserunt illos arma deponere.

XXI

1. Ille (vir) venit. 2. Quid voluit? 3. Cibum voluit. 4. Graccho interfecto, senatores agros suos tenere potuerunt. 5. Agri senatorum revera magni erant. 6. Magnos dolores habuerunt. 7. Multi (viri) servi patriciorum erant.

XXII

1. Scipio milites parat. 2. Columbus naves monstrat. 3. Adherbal in parte orientali Numidiae remanet. 4. Exercitum parat. 5. Rex Africae multos servos habet. 6. Senatus multum aurum a Iugurtha accepit. 7. Auro accepto, senatus contra hunc (virum) pugnare non vult.

XXIII

1. Multas urbes capiunt. 2. Quid in flumen iaciunt? 3. Marius et sui veniunt. 4. Marius at Sulla fortiter pugnant. 5. Magna cum ira dixit. 6. Iugurtha senatum amare simulat, sed revera non amat. 7. Delectu hos (viros) cogunt in exercitum venire.

XXIV

1. Tarquinio expulso, Roma bellum habuit. 2. Patricius nativitate erat. 3. Dicunt quod Iugurtha pacem vult. 4. Dum dubium est, illum legatum revocare nolunt. 5. Non ingenio sed multo labore dictator creatus eat. 6. Nunc cum Communistis pugnant. 7. Etiam boni (viri) pacem aeternam in hoc mundo non habent.

XXV

1. Eidem (viri) veniunt. 2. Marcus eum vidit. 3. Inter cives bellum erat. 4. Potestate Mithradatis non fracta, Sulla in

urbem rursus venit. 5. Sulla enim Marium timuit, et multos amicos Mari interficere voluit. 6. Sulla etiam multa pretiosa Athenis rapuit. 7. Ergo rursus venit ad Italiam navibus suis.

Scramble
Because he feared Marius, Sulla came again into the city. After he took the city, the names of the proscribed were placed by Sulla daily in the Roman forum. Because they were not friends of Sulla, many were killed by Sulla with great butchery.

XXVI
1. Vidit imperatorem qui cum Mithradate pugnavit. 2. Pauci agni ad scholam veniunt. 3. Piratae qui Caesarem ceperunt interfecti sunt. 4. Ii (Ei) qui Sullam oderunt interfecti sunt a viris Sullae. 5. Pompeius erat vir quem piratae non poterant vincere. 6. Lege nova Pompeius magnam potestatem accepit. 7. Ei qui caeci erant non poterant videre.

Scramble
Because he fought bravely, Gnaeus Pompey received the name "Great". Because he was a good general, he also received many extraordinary commands from the Roman senate. In this way, he fought against the pirate who had created a danger on the sea. The same Pompey also led the Jews, who were in the holy land, into the Roman empire.

XXVII
1. Caesar Corneliam in matrimonium duxit. 2. Sulla ira motus est. 3. Necesse erat fugere in montes. 4. Quidam sunt in Italia qui Romam delere volunt. 5. Ipsi hoc facere volunt. 6. Multi in periculum a malis ducti sunt. 7. Caesar se ipsum interficere noluit, Cassius hoc pro eo fecit.

Teacher's Manual

Scramble
Caesar married the daughter of Cinna, whom Sulla did not like. Because he did this, Sulla wanted to kill Caesar. But Sulla should not have wanted to kill Caesar. He (Caesar) had war in his home. For he had a wife. When he had heard this, what did Sulla do? He said that there are many Marius' in that man.

XXVIII
1. Estne Caesar vir qui Galliam in tres partes dividit?
2. Caesar in montes fugit. 3. Viri audaces periculis discunt.
4. Olim erat puella parva quae Maria vocata est. 5. Marcus est vir qui vult Mariam in matrimonium ducere. 6. Marcus in vinculis amoris captus est. 7. Multa pericula acciderunt dum Caesar consul erat.

Scramble
Bibulus remained at home, while Caesar proposed many new laws in the Roman senate.

Caesar in the senate gave great and good speeches, which the senators liked. After the speeches were given, he took an army and led it into Gaul. But Pompey stayed in the city. Caught by the love of Julia, Pompey did nothing at this time against Caesar.

XXIX
1. Hannibal interfici debet. 2. Milites in urbem ducuntur.
3. Artes bonae in schola discuntur. 4. Multi viri boni invidia interficiuntur. 5. Videtur vir bonus esse. 6. Tales viri non in omni terra inveniuntur. 7. Nec in Africa nec in Italia videntur.

Latin by the Natural Method

Scramble

In ancient times, Rome, which even in those days was not a small city, was almost all (totally) captured by the Gauls. And so Caesar, who wanted to have great power, took an army and came into the land which the Gauls held. Caesar came not only into Gaul, but also into another land in which there were fierce men. This land was Germany. Although he conquered all Gaul, in which there were three parts, Caesar did not conquer all Germany.

XXX

1. Caesar in urbem rediit. 2. Pugnare didicit. 3. Tribuni senatui epistolam explicaverunt. 4. Multa praemia militibus dantur. 5. Nunc ad Italiam redeunt. 6. Illa est urbs ex qua navigaverunt. 7. Facile est rem Caesari explicare.

Scramble

The Roman people had given a great privilege to Caesar, because he was a good man, and had done many things for Rome. By this privilege, Caesar was able to seek the consulate although he was in Gaul, not in the city. But a man was moved with envy who should have been a friend to Caesar—Pompey. And so he (this man) asked the Roman people to destroy the privilege of Caesar. When he heard these things, Caesar sent a letter to the senate in which he explained the whole matter.

XXXI

1. Caesar Romam venit. 2. Brundisio navigat. 3. Caesar trans finem meridionalem provinciae suae venit. 4. Caesari loqui conatus est. 5. Fortis apertis, Caesar in oppidum venire potest. 6. Militibus suis qui secuti sunt ipsum (or: eum, or: se) locutus est. 7. Naves nullae Caesari remanserunt.

Teacher's Manual

Scramble

After the tribunes were driven out of Rome, the senate prepared for war. In the southern part of the province that Caesar had, there was a small river which is called the Rubicon. Caesar came across this river with his army. The many but small towns that were in the path of Caesar did not attempt to hold him. With open gates, they received the man whom they said was great. From these towns which, with open gates received Caesar, not a few men followed Caesar.

XXXII

1. Necesse est aut venire aut remanere. 2. Caesar in Thessaliam se recepit. 3. Viri Brundisio redeunt. 4. Multi (viri) in proelio moriuntur. 5. In oppidum se recipere conati sunt. 6. Putat quod Caesar Marco loqui vult. 7. Caesar dixit quod venit, vidit et vicit.

Scramble

They who depart from this life through the gates of death die. Out of all the good things that a man can receive, he should especially ask for a good death from God. For from the future life, no one can go back into this life—nor can he try. For God can do all things that He wants to do without difficulty. For those things which God says always happen. Therefore it is good often to think about this future life which does not have an end. What good is it to Pompey that he was a great general, if he did not have a good death?

XXXIII

1. Dixit quod Caesar veniebat. 2. Cato exercitum colligebat.
3. Exercitus Romanus in Thessaliam sese recipiebat.
4. Caesar, Romam reversus, mox in Africam profectus est.

Latin by the Natural Method

5. Cur ad bellum parabat? 6. Marcus Antonius Caesari coronam monstrabat. 7. Sed hic eam non accipiebat.

Scramble
Although many armies had been conquered in Africa, Caesar was not able to stay in Italy. For Cato, who on those days was the general of an army, did not like Caesar. Although Cato was not a bad general, Caesar was always greater. Therefore he (the latter) quickly conquered him (the former). Soon Caesar set out for Italy. There Mark Anthony was trying (or: kept trying) to give a royal crown to Caesar. He was doing this on a certain feast day on which many men were in the city. But Caesar said nothing about this crown.

XXXIV
1. In Galliam proficiscebatur. 2. Ad pedes eiusdem statuae cecidit. 3. Gladiis et sicis interfectus est. 4. Multi (viri) gladio interficiuntur. 5. Alii pedibus fugiebant. 6. Caesar a vate monebatur. 7. Sed ad pedes Pompeii, cuius inimicus fuerat, cecidit.

Scramble
Not a few senators began to hate Caesar, although he had not accepted the crown from the hands of Mark Anthony. Should they not have loved, and not hated, this great man, who had done many and great things in Gaul for Rome? They should have loved him. Nevertheless, having made no small conspiracy, they tried to prepare death for Caesar. And so on the Ides of March, on which day taxes were once collected in America, Caesar was killed by the daggers at the feet of the statue of Pompey, Now he was at the feet of Pompey at whose feet Pompey had been dead

XXXV

1. Marcus agnum venientem vidit. 2. Audivitne agnum dicentem baa? 3. Marco magistro, Maria laeta est. 4. Dum Caesar vivebat, Brutus non erat laetus. 5. Eum in senatum venientem viderunt. 6. Imperatorem audivit legentem iussa. 7. Melius erat Caesari Roma discedere.

Scramble

In the days of Cicero, the horsemen, since they had much money, did not have to have horses. The Romans, listening to the orations of this Cicero, did not have horse. They were able to understand these even without horses. And so, while the Romans were shouting, Cicero gave many vehement speeches. Although many of those who heard his speeches liked him, Sulla liked neither Cicero himself nor his speeches. Therefore it was better for Cicero to set out from Rome for Greece.

XXXVI

1. Catilina Ciceronem sica interficere conatus est. 2. Dixit quod oderat Ciceronem. 3. Bellum voluit quia multam pecuniam multis debebat. 4. Cur Caesar non est factus rex? 5. Vir est cuius fortitudo magna est. 6. Propter peccata sua puniebatur. 7. Vidit Isabellam pecuniam Columbo dantem.

Scramble

The way to the consulship was difficult for men who were not born in the senatorial class. Certain ones however, among whom was Cicero himself, really did come to this dignity. They who did this were called "new men". In the year in which Cicero was consul there happened that famous conspiracy of Catiline, which Cicero overcame. For this reason, although before this time he had not been humble, Cicero now came into excessive pride. It is said in Sacred Scripture that pride is the beginning of every sin. Although Christians love this virtue, Cicero, who was not a Christian, did not love it.

XXXVII

1. Hi invenientur. 2. Cicero eos is carcerem mittet. 3. Multi illorum (ex illis) qui in coniuratione sunt comprehendentur. 4. De se loquetur. 5. Post hunc diem in urbe non videbuntur. 6. A servis Ciceronis interficientur. 7. Quomodo probabit Cicero quod in coniuratione sunt?

Scramble

Although Fulvia told everything that she had heard about the conspiracy from Curios, Cicero did not want to arrest the conspirators and send them to jail. Although Cicero knew all these things, it was necessary to be able to prove them in court: a thing which Cicero wanted, but could not do. Therefore it was necessary for Cicero to act in other ways. And so in the senate, while many senators were shouting, Cicero gave a violent speech against Catiline. After this speech was given, that Catiline began to be afraid, and left Rome, not without many companions.

XXXVIII

1. A quo accipient milites pecuniam? 2. A Mario, non a Roma. 3. Quis Ciceronem de quo monuit? 4. Catilina dicitur multos interfecisse. 5. Videtur multos consuluisse. 6. Quis quid fecit? 7. Novitne quid fecerunt?

Scramble

Moved by the words of Fulvia, Cicero had given a violent speech against Catiline, by which he forced him to leave the

Teacher's Manual

city. Now moreover, since certain Gauls were providing even written (evidence) about the conspiracy, Cicero came into the senate and asked the senators what he should do about the captured conspirators. The senate decided (it pleased the senate) that those conspirators be killed in prison. Neither Catiline himself nor other conspirators who perhaps were(who happened to be) in the city, were able to give help to those who were condemned in prison. In a great battle against Marcus Petreius, Catiline himself was killed while fighting bravely.

XXXIX

1. Eratne Antonius revera aeger? 2. Reliqui eos liberare conati sunt. 3. Cicero dicit se Catilinam monére. 4. Dixerunt Clodium profanavisse mysteria Bonae Deae. 5. Catilina dicit se vidisse Curium. 6. Cicero dicit non esse necesse habére iudicium publicum. 7. Catilina dicit eos pro vitâ pugnare.

Scramble

The Romans said that this goddess was "the good goddess." Cicero said that Clodius (had) profaned the mysteries of this goddess. But history says that even this "good goddess" was not good. None the less, the Romans, not without truth, said that Clodius was a wicked man. For he was such. Although he bad already become a grown man, Clodius said that he wanted to be adopted by a plebeian family. He said this because he wanted to become tribune of the people. The same Clodius said that Cicero should have given the conspirators a trial before the people—a thing which Cicero actually had not given.

XL

1. In carcerem ibunt. 2. Magno dolore afficientur. 3. Difficile est in exsilium ire. 4. Cur Romam aggrediuntur? 5. Cicero dicit se in magno dolore esse. 6. Habuitne Catilina ius ad iudicium coram populo? 7. Quia haec fecit, dolor magnus ei veniet.

Scramble

History says that the fundamental Roman law, which is called constitutional law, was not written in the days of Cicero. And it is true. But even in these modern times, not all lands have a written constitutional law. Many say that this law is not written in Britain, which is a large island. For this reason, Clodius was able to say that Cicero, who was consul, had acted against the law. Did Clodius speak the truth? It is hard to say.

XLI

1. Ut videret Caesarem venit. 2. In carcerem ducti sunt, ut viri eos interficerent. 3. Cicero in Ciliciam missus est ut esset gubernator ibi. 4. Avunculus Caesaris eum misit ut Ciceronem inveneret. 5. Caesar Ciceroni multa ignovit.
6. Cicero multas orationes ut potestatem Antoni deleret, habuit. 7. Ciceroni nihil dicxt, ne Cicero eum comprehenderet.

Scramble

To force all to come into his camp, Pompey said: "If a man will not fight for me, he will be punished." Roman history says that Cicero came into the camp of Pompey— but that he did practically nothing there. He came into the camp of Pompey because he did not like Caesar, and so that he would not be punished by Pompey. None the less, history

Teacher's Manual

says that Caesar forgave Cicero after the war. After this, Cicero left public life and worked to write many books on philosophical matters. Men in our times read many of these books. These books are also printed.

XLII

1. Milites misit ut Ciceroni loquerentur. 2. Postquam milites discesserunt, Cicero loqui non poterat. 3. Non solum milites, sed etiam Cicero discesserat. 4. Hic vir non est similis illi viro. 5. Vir cui nomina dedit non est amicus eius. 6. Propter odium Antoni, Augustus milites misit ut Ciceronem interficerent. 7. Nomina scripta sunt in foro ut interficerentur.

Scramble

When the triumvirs were fighting among themselves, Cicero gave many violent speeches against Anthony, who was one of the triumvirs, to stir up the Roman people against Anthony. And so, lest he be able to give other such speeches, Anthony asked Octavius to have permission to kill Cicero. Octavius permitted him to be beheaded, although Cicero had done many good things for him. When the soldiers were coming to behead Cicero, the slaves of Cicero tried to defend him. For they said that he had not been a bad man—that he had been good to his slaves.

XLIII

1. Cum Cicero auxilium Augusto dedisset, Augustus Ciceroni auxilium non dedit. 2. Antonius Ciceronem odit, cum Cicero orationes contra ipsum habuisset. 3. Cum Cicero non esset inimicus Romae, gladio interfectus est.
4. Cum Cicero fuisset amicus eius, Augustus eum interfici permisit (permisit ut interficeretur). 5. Antonius dixit

Ciceronem fuisse inimicum Romae. 6. Cum se victum esse vidisset, Antonius seipsum interfecit. 7. Caesar omnia iura Ciceroni reddidit.

Scramble
After he had killed Cicero, Anthony himself was killed. Then a certain man from Gaul (France) said that it was necessary to beware of women, Anthony was not listening. For Anthony thought that he loved Cleopatra, the queen of Egypt. This woman was not really beautiful—for she was fat like the five pigs, our friends. But a certain man said that love was blind—and he spoke the truth. For Anthony, having gathered a great fleet, fought with Octavius. When the great fleet was defeated, Anthony and Cleopatra killed themselves, so that they would not be captured.

XLIV
1. Non erat necesse ut multi Romani et Albani interficerentur. 2. Romanus discessit ne Curiatii ipsum caperent at interficerent. 3. Cum solus esset, Romanus non timebat. 4. Vetus Testamentum docet mundum a Deo creatum esse. 5. Cum omnia fecisset, septimo die Deus requievit. 6. Opus Dei adhuc fit. 7. Cum Christus nasceretur lux magna in caelo venit.

Scramble
Although the Curiatii had killed the other two Horatii, the one Horatius none the less wanted to fight. For although they are in great danger, good Romans will always be brave. That Rome might be saved, many of these brave and good men died. And so in this fight, because of the courage of one Roman, the Romans did not become slaves to the

Teacher's Manual

Albans. For freedom still remains for Rome (or: the freedom of Rome).

XLV

1. Catilina tam malus erat ut Cicero eum non amaret. 2. Caesar Ciceroni ignovit, cum contra ipsum pugnavisset. 3. Cum omnia facta essent, Deus vidit ea esse bona. 4. Deus terrae imperavit ut herbae proferrent. 5. Cum sol et luna facta essent, adhuc non erant animalia in terra.

Scramble

After vegetation was made on the third day. on the fourth day God made the sun and moon. He made these to be in the sky. to give light to the whole world. And so, after many good things had been created, still no creature had come into the world that could love God with good will. So God created the first man from the earth, and the woman from the first man. And then God placed them in paradise.

XLVI

1. Deo obediant ne moriantur. 2. Diabolus interrogat num bonum et malum sciant. 3. Ut hoc comedant non pertnittit eis. 4. Interrogat cur Adam et Eva Deo non obediant.
5. Numquam diabolo credant. 6. Ne se a Deo abscondere conentur. 7. Ne ex ligno scientiae boni et mali comedant.

Scramble

When the first humans had already been created, God ordered (or: God ordered the first humans, when they had been created) not to eat of the fruit of the tree of knowledge of good and evil. While Adam and Eve obeyed the commands of God, they stayed in paradise, having many good things. But the serpent who long before had fallen

Latin by the Natural Method

from the sky because of pride tempted them. "Men will be like gods" said the devil under the form of the serpent.

XLVII
1. Vos mittit ut Catilinam capiatis. 2. Cum peccatum comisissetis, Deus vos ex paradiso misit. 3. Diabolus tam bene loquitur ut ei credamus. 4. Ne credatis diabolo.
5. Potestas Dei tanta est ut vos ab eo abscondere non possitis. 6. Cain tanta voce exclamat ut eum audiamus.
7. Cum Abel pastor esset, agnos obtulit.

Of all the humans who now live on the earth, the mother is Eve, and the father, Adam, They did not obey God, so that they might become like gods. But the devil deceived them. Adam ate the apple offered by his wife; and for this reason they were sent from paradise. Although this happened, God still wanted to give mercy to them. And so a Redeemer is promised by God.

XLVIII
1. In arcam veniamus. 2. Deus tam bonus est ut omnes homines amet. 3. Christus bonus pastor est, et pro agnis morietur. 4. Genus humanum tam malum erat ut Deus eis irasceretur. 5. Magnos misit imbres ut eos deleret.
6. Faciamus navem Noe et filiis eius. 7. Accedit [or Factum est) ut homines pessimi essent diebus Noe.

Scramble
For yourselves and your son make a great ship, which will be an ark—God said this to Noe. For because practically all humans had committed very wicked sins, God sent a flood to destroy them. Great rains came from the skies, and from the sea many waters. For God was angry with exceedingly

Teacher's Manual

great anger because of the sins of very wicked men. But to Noe and his sons, God gave mercy, because they were good.

XLIX

1. Cur in agros venisti cum eo? 2. Te mittit ut aquam feras. 3. Noe, Deus tibi imperat ut arcam facias. 4. Veniamus in arcam cum Noe. 5. Homines tam mali erant ut haec verba audire non possent. 6. Noe, arcam faciebas ut in ea in diluvio navigares. 7. Multa bona tecum habeas.

Scramble

When great waters were coming from the sky and the sea over all the land, many men tried to find a place in which they could be saved, and were not able. For the waters of the great flood came over all the mountains. And they who were in the ark were saved—of the others, no one. After many days, God no longer sent rains, and remembered those who were with Noe in the ark, to bring them from the ark.

L

1. Quid fecistis cum diluvium veniret? 2. In arcam venimus. 3. Cur illam turrem aedificare voluistis? 4. Deus tam bonus est ut in eo confidere debeatis. 5. Altare aedificavimus. 6. Ut turrem aedificemus venimus. 7. Vos interrogavimus cur consilia mutavissetis.

Scramble

Noe, you and your sons should (or: may you) offer sacrifice to God. For he who destroyed all others in the waters, saved you and yours. That you might be able to be saved, he ordered you to make an ark. And when you had come into it, God freed you from all danger. May you trust in Him in whom there is great mercy. And when the bow (rainbow) is seen (will be seen) in the skies, let the promise which God gave come into your mind.

LI

1. Nuntium mitto ut veritatem sciatis. 2. Venisne mecum? 3. Nunc habeo nomen "Abram"—sed Deus nomen meum mutabit, vocabit me "Abraham." 4. In terra Aegypti habito, sed deos Aegypti nescio. 5. Haec terra tam bona est ut non discedamus. 6. Maiores nostri multos deos habuerunt, sed nos unum verum Deum habemus. 7. Turrem non finivimus.

Scramble

God said: "I made all things that are in this world. I wanted to give many good things to all men through Adam and Eve, who were the first humans. You however did not permit me to do the things which I had wanted. Because of your very wicked sins it is necessary that I punish you, although I love you. But nevertheless, a Redeemer will be given to you because of my great mercy.

LII

1. Ex hac terra discedimus quia fames in ea est. 2. Quamquam maiores mei putabant multos deos esse, scio solummodo unum Deum esse. 3. Altare in hoc loco aedificavi quia Deus mihi apparuit. 4. Fames tanta erat ut multi morerentur. 5. Deus mihi dixit quod Hebraei magni erunt. 6. Tam dives est ut nemo eum amet. 7. Videsne stellas? Filii tui maiores numero erunt.

Scramble

The good man Abram, although he was among many polytheists, saw a vision in which God appeared to him, so that he might leave his land. He, to obey the command of God, came into Chanaan. However, because of a famine he came into Egypt, a land in which many and false gods were thought by men to exist. However he loved the one, who is the true God, who also had appeared to him.

LIII
1. Abraham, illi urbi non parcam. 2. Locutus sum, et omnia quae dixi faciam. 3. Manum tuam in altare pone, et promitte quod facies omnia quae te rogabo. 4. Filios nostros circumcidemus quia Deus hoc imperat. 5. Propter Abraham, Deus Hebraeis parcet. 6. Perseverabo rogans Deum ut illi civitati parcat. 7. Veni (venite) nobiscum, et rogabimus Deum ut det nobis auxilium.

Scramble
After Lot was captured, Abram made an army of his slaves, to fight against the four kings. After this victory, Melchisedech offered a sacrifice of wine and bread. When Abraham was living is Mambre (or: to A. living ...) God appeared with two angels. And to him God said that it was necessary to destroy Sodom, because of the very wicked sins. Abraham however continued to ask God not to destroy that city.

LIV
1. Romam imus ut Caesarem videamus. 2. Ciceronem audire nolumus. 3. Vis scire num revertaris. 4. Ibimus ne ignis nos deleat. 5. Surgamus et eamus celeriter ne pereamus. 6. Id quod Deus vult certe nobis bonum est. 7. Certe non manebimus in hoc loco.

Latin by the Natural Method

Scramble

After ten just men had not been found in Sodom, two angels were sent by God to destroy that city. Lot believed them when they spoke of the destruction of the city. However two youths who wanted to marry the daughters of Lot were unwilling to believe him (this one). For Lot said to them: "Let us escape from the ruin of this city, lest we all perish with sinful men.

LV

1. Eamus ut Abraham inveniamus. 2. Nolumus in illo loco remanére. 3. Necesse est ut cum eo loquar. 4. Volo omnia quae rogat facere. 5. Misit me ut veritatem discerem. 6. Cum manum sustulisset, Deus ei imperavit ne filium suum tangeret. 7. Nonne vis me audire?

Scramble

God called Abraham after the birth of his son, commanding that he sacrifice the same son. When all things that were necessary for this sacrifice had been prepared, the father set out with his son for the place which God had pointed out. However before he could kill his son, He ordered Abraham through an angel not to such the prepared victim. God promised that he would give a great blessing to Abraham.

LVI

1. Melius est vidére Caesarem quam vidére quinque porcos. 2. Bonus orator es. 3. Eum saepe audire possumus. 4. Servus sum Abraham, qui vir bonus est. 5. Aquam camelis tuis feram. 6. Semper possumus id facere cui Deus imperat. 7. Voluntas eius semper bona nobis est.

Teacher's Manual

Scramble
Before his death, to provide a good wife for his son, Abraham sent his servant into the land from which he had come. And he asks his master what he should do if the woman will be unwilling to return with him. And he commanded him not to force the woman to come. And the servant set out for Haran, to fulfill the will of the father quickly. He found a good wife for the son, Rebecca, who even gave water for the camels. These things happened by the will of God who is good.

LVII
1. Interrogat num id facere conatus sis. 2. Iacob, cur e terra tua existi? 3. Haec verba locutus sum quia odi eum. 4. Â matre tuâ in Haran missus es. 5. Nescio cur haec locutus sic. 6. Bonis impletus es quia voluntatem Dei implevisti.
7. Esne conatus stellas numerare?

Scramble
Since Jacob had received the blessing which he (Esau) himself had wanted to receive from his Lather, Esau hated him. The mother of Jacob warned him to flee from the house, so that Esau could not kill him. Night found Jacob in an open plain when he was traveling to Haran. And in this place, while sleeping, he saw a great vision from God, of a ladder descending from the sky. Knowing in this way that the place was holy, Jacob gave the name Bethel to the place.

LVIII
1. Loquamur ne in carcerem ponamur. 2. Vos tam boni eratis ut ab omnibus amaremini. 3. Pugnemus fortiter ne moriamur. 4. Unum verum Deum adoremus, non multos deos. 5. Bonis impleamini (implearis). 6. Num servus ero?

7. Inimici me circumsteterunt ut me occidant.

Scramble
There were twelve grandsons of this Isaac, about whom we have already read, that his father was not unwilling to sacrifice him, when God commanded. And among them was Joseph, who had great dreams. He said about one dream: "I saw us binding maniples in the field; and among those maniples (I saw) that mine stood up—but that your maniples were adoring mine." Because of this dream, his brothers were angry at him.

LVIX
1. Conemur discere omnia quae possumus de hac terra.
2. Vir venit. Videamus num multa de hac terra sciat.
3. Loquamur huic viro. 4. In periculo erimus si in hoc loco remanebimus. 5. In carcerem tracti sumus, cum id non meruissemus. 6. Ne fundamus sanguinem eius—eum vendamus his viris. 7. Credentne verbis nostris?

Scramble
The same patriarch also told another dream: that he had seen, as it were, the sun and moon and eleven stars adoring him. On hearing this, the father asked whether he and his mother and brothers should (would have to) adore him on the earth. However although his brothers were angry for this reason, the father of Joseph was not angry. His brothers sold him into Egypt that he might become a slave.

Teacher's Manual

LX

1. Domus magna vocabaris. 2. Audiebaris ab omnibus hominibus in hac terra. 3. Iosephe, emptus es a viris Aegypti. 4. Hanc terram magnam gubernare conabitur. 5. Iosepho loquantur, ipse enim omnia restituet. 6. In hunc locum missus sum crimine falso. 7. Gratiae Pharaonis restitutus es.

Scramble

His father and mother were made very sad, thinking that he had been killed, when really he was a slave in the land of Egypt. Joseph however not only became a slave in that land, but was even sent to prison because of the hatred of the wife of his master. And to him, when he was in prison, the butler and baker of Pharao told their dreams.

LXI

1. Aegyptiis venderis. 2. In terram novam ducor. 3. Si quis vos interrogat, dicite: "Iosephum sequimur." 4. Interrogat num quis velit ipsum videre. 5. Pharao tibi caput tuum auferet, et aves eo pascentur. 6. Interrogavit num quis Iosephi obliviseeretur. 7. Cum rex Iosephum amet, in hac terra remanebimus.

Scramble

Not only men who are in prison can have dreams—for Pharao himself on a certain night bad two dreams which all the soothsayers in the land of Egypt could not interpret: On seeing these dreams, Pharao was terrified, but he did not know that the man who could interpret them was in prison. For the butler whose dream he had once explained in prison, had forgotten Joseph.

LXII

1. A Iosepho servabimur. 2. In domum Pharaonis ducemini (duceris). 3. In locum vestrum restituemini. 4. Tu et amici tui mei obliviscemini. 5. Non occidemur, Rex enim nos amat. 6. Non morabor, sed celeriter proficiscar. 7. Si quid rogabit id facere pollicebor.

Scramble

Pharao placed Joseph, who had interpreted his dream, over all the land of Egypt. For he had explained about the seven years of fertility to come and about the seven other years of famine to come. To show the firmness of his plan, God sent to Pharao two dreams which had the same meaning. Joseph gave orders to the men of the whole land that grain be kept in the cities under the power of Pharao.

LXIII

1. Polliceberisne servare Aegyptum? 2. Id facere conabor.
3. Frumentum in horrea posuit ut servaremur. 4. Scimus cur in carcerem positus sis. 5. Anulo dato, Pharao universae terrae Iosephum praefecit. 6. Sed rex ipse frumentum non habuit: eis ut Iosephum sequerentur imperavit. 7. Venderis quia te odimus.

Scramble

The name of Joseph was changed to another name by Pharao. His new name was: Saphanethphanee. We do not know the meaning of this word, although it is in the Egyptian language which is known to certain modern men. For although they know many things about this language, nevertheless certain things still remain which they cannot translate. St. Jerome thought this name meant: Savior of the world.

Teacher's Manual

LXIV

1. Interrogat cur Aegyptum vincere conati simus. 2. Revera in hanc terram venimus non ut terram vincamus, sed ut frumentum emamus. 3. Cum nos monuerit, eum timere debemus. 4. Haec merito patimur, cum fratrem nostrum vendiderimus. 5. Iosephus discessit ut fleret. 6. Interrogabo eum cur Ikhnaton omnes alios deos delére voluerit. 7. Ut eum nescirent, Iosephus locutus est eis per interpretem.

Scramble

Joseph speaks to his brothers through an interpreter, and asks them from what land they have come and what they want to have. And he commanded them: "Speak the truth to me about all things that you wish, and be prepared to do all things that I tell you. For although to many you seem to be good men, to me you seem to be spies. You have come to make war against us."

LXV

1. Multa sunt facienda. 2. Cur eundum est nobis in Aegyptum? 3. Eundum erit nobis multos dies et multa millia passuum. 4. At frumentum habendum est, aut moriemur.
5. Aegyptii putabant religionem Aton delendam esse.
6. Sequitur ut Osiris etiam non sit deus. 7. Ikhnaton non putabat se ipsum colendum esse.

Scramble

The brothers of Joseph had traveled many miles before they found the money in their sacks. And when it was found they grieved much and said: "What should we do? Should we return to that great man in Egypt? Or (should we return) into our own land? Will we have to lead to him also our youngest brother whom our father loves, Benjamin? Our father will have to grieve if he has to be led."

LXVI

1. Nescimus quis fuerit Pharao qui nescivit Iosephum.
2. Nonne scitis cur Iudaeis nocére voluerit? 3. Multos annos, Iosephus multa bona pro Aegypto fecerat. 4. Nihilominus populus tanta mala passus est ut rogarent Deum ut ipso liberaret. 5. Salus eorum erat in manu (in potentate) Dei.
6. Pharao eos consequi conatus est, sed non potuit.
7. Exercitus regis Aegypti in mari deletus est.

Scramble

The other brothers had dinner with Joseph their brother, whom they did not recognize. But when the time came to depart, Joseph ordered money put into their sacks again. But to see whether they were till moved by envy, he ordered his own silver cup to be put secretly into the sack of Benjamin. The ministers of Joseph, when they had caught up with them, asked where they had put the cup. When it was found in the sack of Benjamin, they grieved much.

LXVII

1. Eamus in Aegyptum ad frumentum emendum.
2. Exercitus celeriter venit ad Iudaeos capiendos. 3. Deus autem Aegyptios in mare duxit ut eos deleret. 4. Iosepho non erat pecunia quando in Aegyptum venit. 5. Nunc multa bona sunt ei. 6. Iosephus iussit pecuniam poni in saccos eorum ad eos probandos. 7. Deus misit eum in Aegyptum ad fratres servandos.

Teacher's Manual

Scramble
Joseph did all these things to test his brothers. He did not persecute the brothers to punish those who had deserved to be punished. For Joseph did not have envy as they did. For they, because of ill will had wanted to harm him, by selling him as a slave into a foreign land. He however gave them good for evil, to save them.

LXVIII
1. Iosephus in Aegyptum missus est saluti fratribus.
2. Multae nationes vincendae erant antequam Iudaei in Palaestinam inirent. 3. Remanendo in Aegypto Iosephus vir magnus factus est. 4. Amor regendi multos delevit.
5. Iosephus fratribus ignovit. 6. Servo erat regi. 7. Iacob gravis aetate erat, sed magnus bonis operibus.

Scramble
And when Joseph saw that his brothers no longer had a desire of harming, he confessed that he was their brother; "I am your brother, whom you sold into Egypt. You should not fear—for the God of our fathers sent me to this land to save you. Moreover, God gave me the will of forgiving you what you have done. I will give an abundance of all good things to you."

LXIX
1. Prophetiam audituri sumus. 2. Dicit haec nobis ventura esse in novissimis diebus. 3. Septuaginta dies fleverunt. 4. Iacob eis dedit prophetiam Iudaeos suos duces habituros donec Christus veniret. 5. Iacob vidit mortem mox venturam esse. 6. Placuit Pharaoni Hebraeos iuvare. 7. Iosephus ad patrem videndum cucurrit.

Latin by the Natural Method

Scramble

Joseph told Pharao that his father would come, and asked Pharao for many things for his brothers. And he ordered him to give them very good land. For it pleased Pharao to help the brothers and father of Joseph. But before his death, Jacob the father of Joseph was to give a great prophecy about things to come. Among other things, he predicted several things about the future Messias; (he said) that he was to be sent when there was no longer a leader from Juda.

LXX

1. Mesopotamiae diluvia habenda sunt ad terram irrigandam. 2. Amor regendi periculum est multis hominibus. 3. Ad exercitum alendum, multus cibus habendus est. 4. Nemo adest praeter nos Aegyptios. 5. Iacob dixit Christum venturum esse. 6. Iosephus dixit Iudaeos ex Aegypto discessuros esse. 7. Fratres timebant ne Iosephus ipsos puniret.

Scramble

Joseph set out with many of the elders from Egypt to bury his father in the land of his fathers. For Jacob, when about to die, had asked Joseph for a tomb in that land. However after this, his brothers feared he might have a desire (will) to punish them. And they, in fear approached him, and asked him not to be angry.

LXXI

1. Gilgamesh ferocior Humbabâ est. 2. Eratne ille rex ferocissimus in mundo? 3. Iudaei crescebant et facti sunt maiores numero Aegyptiis. 4. Iosephus gratior patri suo erat ceteris fratribus. 5. Currendo celeriter ab inimicis suis

evasit. 6. Marcus est fortis, Iulius fortior, et Augustus fortissimus omnium est. 7. Auctoritas regis non est contemnenda.

Scramble
By forgiving their sins, Joseph showed them that he was better than they. After his death, the Hebrews, by growing swiftly, became very numerous. Even though they were not more numerous than the Egyptians themselves, they gave reason to fear. And the king himself feared lest they go over to his enemies. For this reason, the king ordered that infants should be killed soon after their birth.

LXXII
1. Erantne multa cornua Humbabae? 2. Gilgamesh desiderabat immortalitatem plus quam aliquid aliud. 3. Etiam conatus est cum magico somno pugnare, et bene pugnavit, sed somnus melius pugnavit. 4. In genibus subrogavit Utanapistim vitam, aeternum. 5. Via moriendi omnibus nota est, at via vivendi in aeternum non est notus eis. 6. Gilgamesh hoc clare non vidit; ausus est ergo fortiter contra mortem pugnare. 7. Omnes homines dixerunt Gilgamesh: "Mors est onus grave quod dii hominibus dederunt nulla est spes evadendi."

A certain daughter of the Hebrews, who was the sister of Moses, dared to speak to the daughter of Pharao. For she, bending the knee to the Egyptian girl, asked whether she wished a woman of the Hebrews to be called to care for the boy. And when she ordered it, the sister of Moses ran quickly to her (his) mother. In this way he lived in the palace of the king of Egypt, and was taught the wisdom of Egypt.

Latin by the Natural Method

LXXIII

1. Si Gilgamesh herbam invenerit (inveniet) in aeternum vivet. 2. Si eam non custodit, serpens eam capiet. 3. Ergo serpentes nunc habent potestatem non moriendi. 4. Estne Gilgamesh multo melior serpente? 5. Quidam ex civibus quos regit putant non (eum non esse meliorem). 6. Si populus non crediderit (credet), quid faciam? 7. In mare iit ad herbam quaerendam.

LXXIV

1. Dii concilium habuerunt et diluvium miserunt ad genus humanum delendam. 2. Si Ea Utanapistim non monuerit (monebit), hic etiam delebitur. 3. Aaron obviam venit ei in deserto. 4. Moyses non intellexit cur rubus incolumis remansit (remaneret). 5. Eratne Bel multo major deus quam Ea? 6. Dii sicut muscae descenderunt ad sacrificium capiendum. 7. Utanapistim ex periculo moriendi in diluvio evasit.

LXXV

1. Si Ea non monuisset eum, Utanapistim mortuus esset. 2. Plurimi dei eum occidere maluissent. 3. Si Bel navem videat, deleatne eam? 4. Si sacrificia non haberent, quid facerent? 5. Gilgamesh dicit: "Si immortalis essem, laetus essem.
6. Pharao cederet si veritatem de Deo sciret. 7. Si Pharao me videre vult (voluerit; volet), me vocet.

LXXVI

1. Navibus delendis, Romani Carthaginem vicerunt. 2. Dii de omnibus hominibus delendis locuti sunt. 3. Ars hominum regendorum difficilior est. 4. Pulvere percutiendo, Aaron multa millia cinifum eduxit. 5. Si Pharao Deum timuisset, cor suum non induravisset. 6. Si Hebraei in Gessen non

fuissent, habuissentne cinifes? 7. Deus maluit Moysen mittere ad populum suum liberandum miraculis faciendis.

LXXVII

1. Non licebat eis ex Aegypto discedere. 2. Necesse erat ut Moyses plures plagas mitteret. 3. Bello, in hoc loco manére nolumus: discedere malumus. 4. Pharaoni dimittere statuit, at deinde cor suum induravit iterum. 5. Multis plagis, Hebraei Deum timuerunt. 6. Vix evasit Moyses a morte in populo servando? 7. Quod si Aaron terram non percussisset virga cinifes non venissent.

LXXVIII

1. Si Pharao non peccavisset, plagae non venissent. 2. Cur placuit ei permittere ut Israel discederet? 3. Pharao eos labore non liberavit. 4. Pharao peccatum suum auxit indurando corde 5. Fulgur quale numquam antea visum est in Aegypto, super omnem terram venit. 6. Cum Moyses manum suam tetendisset, tonitruum cessavit. 7. Fulgur in omni terra visum est, excepta parte in quâ habitabant Hebraei.

LXXIX

1. Multi viri magni erant Romae et Athenis. Caesar a Bruto occisus est. 2. Sica occisus est. 3. Si non desideravisset rex esse, essetne interfectus? 4. Pharao dixit se non velle ultra vidére faciem Moysis. Deus fulgur in omnem terram Aegypti misit, ita ut populus terreretur. Peccatis Pharaonis, decem plagae in terram venerunt.

LXXX

1. Cum Pharao filium suum mortuum esse vidisset, Moysen et Aaron vocavit. 2. Dixit eis se permissurum esse ut Israel

iret. 3. Unusquisque paravit ut discederet ex Aegypto nocte. 4. Cum agnum comedissent, sanguinem eius in postes imposuerunt. 5. Aegyptii ab angelo Domini sunt occisi.
6. Sanguine agni, angelus Iudaeos non occidit. 7. Agno sacrificando, Iudaei sunt servati.

LXXXI

1. Quomodo potiti sunt Iudaei terra sancta? 2. Omnibus rebus quae Dominus eis dederat fructi sunt. 3. Ne unum quidem eis deerat. 4. Si Domino bene servissent, in hoc loco remansissent. 5. Bene uti debemus omnibus quae Deus nobis dedit. 6. Cum holocaustum non esset siccum, ignis de caelo super id descendit voravitque. 7. Dominus magnopere laudandus est.

Teacher's Manual

KEY TO SCRAMBLES AND ENGLISH TO LATIN OF BOOK II

VIII

The priests who were carrying the ark entered the Jordan. When the priests' feet had touched the water, the river became dry. When Josue had seen this, he called to him twelve men, whom he had chosen from the sons of Israel, And he ordered them to gather twelve stones which would be placed for a monument (to be placed for....)

IX

In order that he might he able to conquer, before night, the wicked enemies who were fighting against the people of Israel.. Josue the General said to the sun: Sun, do not move towards Gabaon, so that we may be able to capture our enemies. He therefore, when he had captured the enemy whom he was pursuing, also killed the kings of the enemy, lest they be able to fight again against the people whom the Lord loved.

X

The Jews offended the Lord their God, who had freed them from the land of Egypt through Moses, who was a holy man. The Lord God handed them over to the Madianites who were making invasions into Palestine every year. When God had done this, the people who were humbled cried to Him. And He,to save His people, sent a great Judge to them.

1. Iudices Iudaei non erant in foro; magni duces erant. 2. In diebus Gedeon, Dominus Iudaeos in manu Madianitarum tradiderat. 3. Hoc fecit quia filii Israel in conspectu Domini

Latin by the Natural Method

peccaverant. 4. Madianitae venerunt vecti camelis et incursiones in Iudaeos faciebant.

XI

Lest Israel should boast against the Lord saying, "I was freed by my own strength, the Lord commanded the Judge Gideon to send many men home. Gideon did not send home those whom he saw licking the water from their hands. When he had done this the Lord of Israel, who in powerful, gave victory to him. After the jars were struck together. all the enemies who had come against the people whom God loved, were conquered.

1. Gedeon etiam vocabatur [dicebatur] Ierobaal. 2. Si Domino non obediet (-iverit), Madian in manu eius non tradetur. 3. Dominus imperavit ei ut in castra hostium nocte descenderet. 4. Cum venisset, virum somnium narrantem audivit.

XII

Samson had not told the truth to Dalila, whom he loved greatly. And when she had often seen that he had not told the truth, she became troublesome even to the man who was the bravest in all Israel. And he was conquered by a woman, whom he thought he loved, although he had even torn apart a lion which he came upon as a boy.

1. Quae mulier erat quam Samson amavit? 2. Dalila mulier erat Philistinorum quae Samson saepe interrogavit et molesta erat ei. 3. Per tres vices Samson Dalilae mentitus est. 4. Spectantibus fere tribus millibus utriusque sexus, Samson Dominum invocavit. [Alternative: *Cum spectavissent*]

Teacher's Manual

XIII

The Philistines feared the sons of Israel, because they shouted with a great cry after the ark of God came into the camp. Nevertheless, because he had not admonished his sons, the priest who was called Heli had to die. Really the father should have warned his sons, who did that which they should not have done. And so the Philistines took the ark which the sons of Israel were not allowed to touch, if they were not Levites. Because they did not know the danger, the enemies of Israel took the ark without fear into a place into which it should not have been taken. They who did this had to be punished by the Lord.

1. Rex inveniendus est Iudaeis. 2. Multos annos Dominus rex eorum fuerat, eosque multa millia passuum per desertum duxerat. 3. Quis petunt, hoc faciendum est Samueli. 4. Filii monendi sunt sacerdoti Heli. 5. Multos annos filii eius malum fecerunt in conspectu Domini.

XIV

Because the asses that belonged to the father of Saul had been lost, Saul himself was sent to seek them. And he, when he had hunted for many hours and had not found them, thought he-should return to Ms father, leet his father be worried. After he had learned from Samuel, who was a great prophet, that they had been found, he also heard that he was to be anointed king, because the people of Israel had asked for a king. However not all the sons of Israel thought they should give gifts to him whom Samuel had made king.

1. Huic regi multum aurum; illi regi magnus exercitus. 2. Cis filium suum ad asinas reperiendas misit. 3. Samuel venit ad ungendum eum in regem. 4. Samuel populum convocavit ad

annuntiandam legem regis. 5. Adsunt ad prophetam audiendum.

XV

(One) should not fight against the Lord, but should always obey His words. For David, by obeying His voice, although he had been only a boy who fed the sheep, became the king of the people of God. David was sent to save his people at the time when Goliath, who was a low born man, was reproaching them. And he went down to fight against Goliath without fear, protected not by great armor, but by the favor of God.

1. David auxilio venit fratribus suis. 2. Non parcetur viro malo. 3. Semper obediendum est verbis Dei. 4. Regi non ignoscetur. 5. Goliath egrediebatur ad exprobrandum exercitui Israel.

XVI

When he had heard the words of Goliath, who reproached the army of Israel, David, who was still a boy, said that he would go out against him. Intending to ask God for fortitude, David therefore prayed. But Goliath surely thought that he would kill this boy who had come down to fight him with a sling (and) without arms. By saving this boy who trusted in God, the Lord wished to teach us all wisdom.

1. Videtur interfecturus esse Goliath. 2. Dixit se hoc facturum esse. 3. Difficile est docere homines sapientiam.
4. David solummodo fundam et baculum rogavit, pugnaturus contra Goliath. 5. Audiamus eum, rogaturus est enim pacem.

XVII

The women who came out from all the cities of Israel said that the holy man David. who, although he had been a boy, had killed Goliath. was greater than Saul. Saul. who was king, thought that he was the greatest, and not less than this youth. For at the time at which he was chosen as king by Samuel, whom the Lord Himself had sent, the same Saul seemed to all the people to be taller and better (or: seemed taller and better than all the people). Therefore a greater danger came to David from Saul than there had been from Goliath.

1. Puto David meliorem esse quam regem; aliqui (or: quidam) putant eum optimum esse. 2. Putasne Ionathan futururn esse fortiorem quam amicum suum? 3. Saul lugens dixit inimicum suum iustiorem esse se (quam se). 4. David seipsum minorem pulice putat. 5. Dominus virum sanctiorem saluti populo suo mittet.

XVIII

David, who really was much braver than Saul, wished to spare Saul, although he was able to strike him quickly, lest he touch the anointed one of the Lord. Therefore although Saul had acted badly against him, David dealt (acted) better with him. Nevertheless David thought he should leave, lest Saul try to kill him. And so he whom Saul feared came into the land of the Philistines—going forth from which he might fight bravely against Araalec.

1. David Deo fidelissime obedivit multo fidelius quam rex.
2. Clarius quam Saul id quod bonum erat vidit. 3. David multo fortius quam ceteri pugnavit. 4. Rex promisit se bene facturum esse. 5. Regem paulo plus quam alii iuvit.

XIX

Would all the land that Saul ruled have come into the power of the Philistines if he had always obeyed the Lord? If he whom the Lord had chosen to be king over the people of Israel had not acted so wickedly in the sight of the Lord, the sons of Israel would be in peace, not in captivity. If David himself had attempted to build the temple after the Lord had given a prophecy through Nathan that a son of David would build the temple to the Lord, perhaps it (he) would not have pleased the Lord.

1. Si contra voluntatem Domini facere velit, ei non placeat.
2. Si Saul Samuelem exepectavisset, Deus eum non reiecisset. 3. Non essemus in potestate Philistinorurn si David rex esset. 4. Si male facit, puniendus est. 5. Si ante Dagon genu flectat, Dominus eum non iuvet.

XX

By taking for himself the wife of Urias, David sinned against the Lord who had so often saved him. Although David had written so many things in the psalms (which he wrote because he really loved God) about doing the will of God, he himself did evil in the sight of the same Lord. The same king committed also another great sin by placing the husband of this woman in a most dangerous spot in war. Nevertheless the Lord, who is always good, said He preferred rather to forgive than to punish.

1. Sollicitandis cordibus virorum Israel Absalom potestatem accepit. 2. Viris ad se vocandis, melior quam rex esse videbatur. 3. De hominibus omnibus iuvandis multa locutus est. 4. His faciendis, se meliorem esse monstravit, ita ut eum mallent. 5. Si veritatem scivissent, David maluissent.

Teacher's Manual

XXI

Because of his promise, which he had previously given, when Bathsheba asked, David caused (made) Solomon, who was the son of Bathsheba, to reign in place of himself. It always pleased the king to do that which he had previously promised. For David said that it was right to act in such a way, lest he act wickedly. Therefore, after Solomon his son had been placed upon the king's mule, when they came to Gihon, a horn of oil was taken up and the shout was raised: Long live king Solomon.

1. Corde sapienti eius, multi ad Salomonem audiendum veniebant. 2. Regnante Salomone, populus liber erat timore inimicorum. 3. Licebat ei donum a Deo petere. 4. Volebat sapientiam petere. 5. Si semper in viis Domini ambulavisset, Dominus eum multis non privavisset.

XXII

A message (messenger) was sent by Solomon, who wanted to build the temple, to Hiram, who lived at Tyre and was king there. Solomon asked that cedars of Lebanon be cut by the servants of Hiram and sent by sea to him. In the following centuries, even at Rome, which later became the head of the whole world, a greater and more beautiful temple was seen by no one. When it was finished, the king carried out the dedication not without many sacrifices.

1. Hiram rex erat Tyri, Hierosolymis regnabat Salomon.
2. Multa sacrificia a sacerdotibus oblata sunt. 3. Oves gladiis interfecerunt. 4. Nube magna, aliae oves offerri a sacerdotibus non potuerunt. 5. Si Salomon fidelis fuisset, regnum non esset divisum a Deo.

XXIII

When Jeroboam ruled in the northern kingdom, in the southern kingdom there was a king who preferred to make heavier the yoke that Solomon had made very heavy: Roboam. Since the advice of the men who had given good counsels to his father Solomon had not pleased him, all but one tribe went away from him. The Lord through a man of God, commanded the king of the southern kingdom, when he wanted to gather the whole house of Jude to make war against Israel, not to do this.

1. Cum Achab regnum septentrionale rexit Elias viduam vidit. 2. Cum fere nullum cibum haberet, panem Eliae dedit. 3. Cum filius eius mortuus esset, vidua Eliae locuta est.
4. Cum venerit Elias filium meum servabit. 5. Cum videbit eum vivere, vidua laeta erit.

XXIV

Performing his duty, which the Lord had commanded him, Elias gathered all the prophets who ate of the table of Jezabel. When the false prophets had tried to ask help of Baal, Elias offered the sacrifice, using the fire which the Lord sent from heaven. Afterwards, when the same prophet who bad done this had asked the Lord, the whole land enjoyed the rain which it desired.

1. Nemo carnibus sacrificii quod Elias obtulit vescebatur. 2. Multi carnibus frui volebant. 3. Cum Elias Deum rogasset, ignis omnem carnem consumpsit. 4. Cum Eliseus Eliae ministrasset, pallio eius potitus est. 5. Si Eliseus eum ascendentem viderit (videbit), spiritum eius habebit.

Teacher's Manual

XXV

Because king Achaz was sinning the Lord promised that He would give a sign through Isaias, who was the greatest prophet in the kingdom of Juda, to which the Lord had promised help. Although the prophet promised (it), the king said that he was unwilling by asking a sign to tempt the Lord who had promised a sign. Since he was unwilling to ask, the prophet Isaias, who was sent, spoke a prophecy which said that Christ would come. The Assyrians however boasted when the king who had not listened to the prophet, paid tribute.

1. Confidente in Domino rege Ezechia, Ierusalem in manus Assyriorum non tradita est. 2. Sennacherib sagittam in Jerusalem non misit cum angelus Domini eam protegeret. 3. Visis corporibus mortuorum, Sennacherib abiit. 4. Dicente Deum venturum esse propheta, multi Iudaei non intellexerunt. 5. Nolente obedire rege, urbs obsessa est.

XXVI

When Josias, who was devout, was king, the end of the empire of Assyria came. After king Assurbanipal, who was a learned man, had died, three kings who were not so great came onto the throne of the land which had once terrified many nations lest they wish to resist. Because the generals who had come from once-conquered land, besieged (it), the city of Ninive was broken, so that it fell. When the city that had been proud was captured, the kings who had conquered divided the land among themselves.

1. Regnantibus regibus potentibus, Assyria aliis gentibus terrori fuerat. 2. Rogante qui ex semine regio erat Daniele,

servus regis legumina ad vescendum portavit. 3. Completis sicut rex imperaverat diebus, adducti sunt ad regem.
4. Capta urbe, Nabuchodonosor omnes thesauros templi Babylonem attulit. 5. Legumina cibo illis erant.

XXVII

When the order had gone forth from the king that the wise men should be killed, Daniel prayed to the God of heaven who reveals secrets to men who trust in God. For the king, since he had forgot the dream which he saw, had asked both the dream and the interpretation from those who seemed to be wise, but were not. And they answered him that what he asked was impossible. However that which seemed impossible to men, because they were men, was easy for Daniel who trusted in the true God.

1. Somnium oblitus, rex territus est. 2. Audito sapientium responso, rex inane est. 3. Egressa sententia, Daniel regem ut tempus daret rogavit. 4. Somnium interpretatus, Daniel magna dona accepit. 5. In Deo confisus[1], Daniel non est interfectus.

XXVIII

History says that a certain Babylonian king who loved Daniel was forced to hand over Daniel by priests who were shouting because Daniel had killed the dragon. The same king found him still alive on the seventh day although he had been put into the den of lions. The Lord sent food to the same Daniel, while he was staying in the lion's den, through a prophet who was carried by an angel. But the evil

---

[1] NB: Confido, confidere, confisus is semi-deponent.

priests who had spoken against Daniel, when they were put into the same den, were devoured at once.

1. Cyrus qui Babylonem vicit urbem ingressus dixit deum Marduk ipsum misisse. 2. In Babylonia multos Iudaeos invenit qui, ducti illuc ab aliis regibus, redire voluerunt.
3. Homines qui in Samaria habitabant, videntes Iudaeos templum aedificare, auxilium dare voluerunt. 4. Iudaei qui in captivitate fuerant regressi templum aedificare voluerunt.

XXIX

When the Jews had begun to build the temple because of the edict which he who was king of the Medes and Persians had given, the man who, after being appointed general by the Persians, had seen them working, tried to stop those who were building. Those who wanted to build the temple said to him that they were doing so because of the edict of Cyrus, who also had permitted them to return to their own land. When the appointed general had heard these things, he sent a letter to the king of the Persians to learn his will.

1. Volentes templum aedificare convenerunt. 2. Dux a Persis constitutus ad laborantes venit. 3. Auxilium datum est a rege aedificantibus. 4. Anno sexto regis Darii templum ab aedificantibus completum est. 5. Dicentes Darium malum esse veritatem non dicunt.

XXX

All those who served the king bent the knee when they saw Aman, whose throne was exalted above all the princes whom the king had. Those who adored pleased this man who was not without pride. Aman was very angry because Mardochaeus, who was a Jew, was unwilling to adore. And he, having returned to the palace, asked the king that all the people, from whom Mardochaeus had come, might perish. After he had heard the petition, the king gave the edict to him who asked.

1. Puellae cum audissent flentes Reginae Esther nuntiaverunt. 2. Regina autem, cum Mardochaeo locuta, se non comesuram esse tres dies et tres noctes dixit.
3. Mardochaeus dixit forsan illa in palatium missam esse saluti Iudaeis. 4. Regina ingressa locum in quo sedebat rex territa est.

XXXI

The king said that Queen Esther would obtain what she wished even if she asked a half of all the lands that he had: [he said] that he really loved the queen, and that he would do all that she, whom he had chosen queen, wanted. And to him the queen [said]: that she did not want great things, and that she did not ask half of the whole kingdom, but her own life and the safety of many who were in the people from which she had come. When these thing had been heard, there came into the mind of the man who was with them, a suspicion: that the king would do something against him, that perhaps he would even kill him.

1. Senex se non comesurum esse carnes porcina dixit.
2. Etiam alias carnes non accepit: iuvenes putaturos esse ipsum peccasse contra legem Dei. 3. Primus fratrum ad regem ductus est: se paratum esse mori magis quam leges patrias praevaricari. 4. Secundus frater venit: Deum mundi regem suscitaturum esse in vitam aeternam legibus suis obedientes.

Teacher's Manual

XXXII

History tells that Alexander, who became a very great general when he was still young, captured all Persia. [it says:] that he gathered an army from all the Greek states that he might set out against the king of Persia. [It says] that he, after fighting many very great battles in the land into which he had come, conquered even the great king of Persia himself. [It says:] that he led his army to the boundaries of India and that he wanted to go on to eastern lands, but that he was not able. [It says:] that he said that the army in which he trusted did not want to conquer India.

1. Filius secundus etiam recusavit regi obedire; se velle legibus patriis obedire. 2. Filius tertius venit: se propter lege Dei corpus suum despicere. 3. Antiochum non habiturum resurrectionem bonam dixit filius quartus. 4. Mater filium ultimum spectavit: eum debére aspicere ad coelum at terram, et intelligere Deum ea fecisse ex nihilo.

XXXIII

The devout brave men who had gathered to obey the law struck the wicked Jews who had gone over to the law of the gentiles because they did not trust in God. The nations that had come against the Jews, seeing the great victories that they won, were afraid. Matthathias said that they should remember the good works which (their fathers) had done in their own generations. They believed that they should not listen to the words of men who sinned against the law of God.

1. Boni in multis quas habent tentationibus viri sunt fideles. 2. Omnibus in se confidentibus Deus auxilium dat. 3. Multa sicut timuerunt mala super eos venerunt. 4. Iniqui qui ad

legem transierunt gentium viri ad Matthathiam non venerunt. 5. Magna sicut promiserat potestate Deus eos salvavit.

XXXIV

The evil king who was feeling severe torments in his entrails wrote: "I wish the best health to the best citizens whom I have." "Wishing to provide for the common welfare, as I should, I have written to my good son, whom I love, that he may take on the great kingship which I can no longer bear. May you therefore be mindful of the many benefits which I have already given, and of the great benefits which my son is about to give."

1. Quod amaverunt sanctuarium viderunt desertum.
2. Pessimus quem timebamus inimicus noster mortuus est.
3. In magnam ingressus est urbem ut magnos sicut desiderabat thesauros caperet. 4. Pessimo regis qui superbus fuerat odore gravatus est exercitus. 5. Se sanctum optimis ornaturum muneribus templum pollicetur.

XXXV

He who had been appointed by Antiochus leader of the army of Syria saw—not without fear—the army coming to him. The man who had been appointed leader by Antiochus said to the man who was coming that he would give him the city of Ptolemais: for he had come for that reason. The citizens of the same city, who were wicked, seized him when he came into the city because he believed the leader, In Judea itself, those who heard all thing that were done, were not happy.

Teacher's Manual

1. Credentes duci capti sunt. 2. Dabo, inquit, venienti mecum multa bona. 3. Ingredientes gladio interfecerunt. 4. Verba haec dicentium non erant vera. 5. Sequentes Ionathan pauci erant.

****

HOW DO YOU SAY IT DEPARTMENT

<u>Adversative clauses</u>: Cum solummodo tres dies iter fecissent, contra Moysen murmuraverunt. Quamquam in deserto erant, aquam habére poterant. Cum Deus eis coturnices misisset, ei non bene servierunt. Quamvis Justus Deus sit, ob hanc murmurationem eos non punivit. Deum qui bonus eis sit non amant.

<u>Causal clauses</u>: Quin Deus descendet, populus non debet in montem ascendere. Moysen quippe qui in monte cum Deo fuisset timuerunt. Cum Moyses moram fecisset in monte, ad Aaron venerunt, Aaron vitulum conflatilem fecit quia populus rogasset. Deus eos non delevit quod Moyses oravit.

<u>Conditional clauses</u>: Si Moyses non oravisset, Dominus Deus eos delevisset. Si Domini sunt, filii Levi hoc facient. Si Moyses adesset vitulum conflatilem non coleremus. Si nos videat (viderit), quid dicat? Si non oravisset pro nobis, non adessemus.

<u>Result clauses</u>: Core tam superbus erat ut Moysen non timeret. Non erat qui obedire vellet. Non erat dignus qui incensum in ignem coram Domino poneret. Nemo potest Dominus blasphemare quin puniatur. Terra eos deglutivit ita ut etiam hodie corpora eorum non sint inventa.

Latin by the Natural Method

Substantive result clauses: Accidit ut Moyses petram bis percuteret. Moyses effecit ut aqua de petra veniret. Aquam de petra fluere fecit. Deus effecit ut serpentes igniti in populum venirent. Accidit ut sanarentur aspicientes in serpentem aeneum.

Clauses w. verbs of doubt: Non est dubium quin Iosue fuerit servos Moysis fidelis Moysen dubitaverat num aqua ventura esset de petra. Non est dubium quin Dominus in manus nostras totam terram hanc dederit. Ob dubitationem eius, in terram quam Deus filiis Israel dedit non ingresses est. Dubitasne quin Moyses in Monte Nebo mortuus sit?

Clauses with verbs of fearing: Ne timeatis ne Deus Iordanem nobis non siccet. Populus Iericho timuerunt ne filii Israel urbem caperent. Sacerdotes arcam portantes non timuerunt ut aquae siccarentur. Viri Iericho timuerunt ne Deus urbem ipsorum traderet. Non tamen timuerunt ne muri urbis corruerent.

Purpose clauses: Deus de caelo magnos misit Lapides ut hostes percuterent. Sol at luna in caelo steterunt ne hostes evaderent. Viros misit qui quinque reges caperent. Reges sese in spelunca absconderunt ne viderentur. Deus lucem prolongavit quo facilius hostes sequerentur.

Substantive Volitive clauses: Hortabatur servarent omnia quae in libro legis scripta sunt. Eos rogavit ne deis alienis servirent. Gedeon Madianitas vincere voluit. Angelus ei imperat ut altare Baal deleat. Ioas populum monuit ne filium ipsius interficerent.

Teacher's Manual

<u>Clauses w. verbs of hindering</u>: Deus non recusavit quin signum Gedeoni daret. Nihil impedire potest quin Deus faciat voluntatem suam. Parvus numerus virorum non prohibet eos vincere. Deus vetat Gedeonem assumere viginti duo millia virorum. Somnium duos Madianitas ne pugnarent impedivit.

<u>Proviso clauses</u>: Tibi narrabo dummodo Philistinis hoc ne dicas. Coram to Iudam modo me ad columns quibus tota nititur domus ducas. Mori non recusabo tantum ut multi Philistini mecum moriantur.

<u>Relative clauses</u>: Anna ut quae ad Dominum oravisset filium accepit. Heli filios suos qui partes sacrificiorum sumpsissent non punivit. Deus Ophni et Phinees qui cum contempsissent punivit. Nemo erat qui Samuelem non honoraret. Omnium prophetarum quos quidem cognoverim ille piissimus est.

<u>Temporal clauses I</u>: Cum Philisthini vocem clamoris magni in castris Hebraeorum audissent, timuerunt. Simul ac arca in castra venit, exclamavit populus. Cum mane surrexissent, Dagon iacentem super faciem suam invenerunt. Cum Dagon vidissent, Deum Israel timuerunt. Exercitus ad castra veniebat cum equos hostium vident (viderunt). Dum pugnabant orabat. Dum iter tacit, altare Dagon vidit.

<u>Temporal clauses II</u>: Regem eis non dedit donec regem petiverant (petissent) Etiam ante hoc tempus regem desideraverant. Samuel Saulem non unxit donec Deus eum hoc facere iussit (iussisset). Antequam hoc accidit, Saul erat solummodo filius novissimae tribus Israel. Antequam peteret, Samuel ei omnia quite in corde eius erant indicavit.

Latin by the Natural Method

<u>Substantive clauses</u>: Quod Saul rex erat quibusdam non placuit. Quod eum despexerunt, dissimulabat se audire. Quid quod munera ei non dederunt?

<u>Impersonal Verbs</u>: Saul, non licet tibi holocaustum offerre. Regi Amalec non nocitum est a Saule. Parsum est ei. Bethelehem ventum est. Samuelem itineris non piguit. Salus populi Israel magnopere Sarnuelis intererat. Or, better: Hoc magnopere Samuelis intererat, ut salus esset populo Israel. Samuelem paenituit quod Deus Saulem reiecerat.

<u>Independent Subjunctives</u>: Audeat vir unus ex Israel solus mecum pugnare! Videres Goliath quotidie egredi. Vellem contra emu pugnare. Viri Israel dixerunt: Quid faciamus? Hic enim vir decem pedum est. Goliath dixit: Utinam ne (or: non) cum David pugnassem. Me Deus adiuvet in hac pugna. Non ausi essemus cum Goliath pugnare. Hoc ne faciat.

<u>Possessive case</u>: Multum periculi. Satis praemii. Tantum negotii. Nihil bona. Si quid mali. Plurimum boni. Minus laboris. Fastidiens studiorum. Expers rationis. Multarum rerum peritus. Consilii particeps. Viri fortis est pro patria mori. Avari est pecuniam amare. Hoc parvi est. Quinque denariis constat. Homicidii eum accuso. Multae magnae eum damnat. Marci memini. Oblitus sum pecuniae meae.

<u>Dative case</u>: Viginti viros auxilio nobis misit. Hoc nobis exemplo erit. Multa pecunia est ei. Nobis multi amici sunt. Nocetur finis Israel. Nobis a Domino parcitur. Mihi persuadetur. We must come. I must fight. Ille tibi interficiendus est. Nobis eundum est.

Teacher's Manual

<u>Objective case</u>:   Quinque annos remansit. Quinque millia passuum venit. Gladius duo pedes longus est. Agrigentum venimus. Rus venit.

<u>Ablative case</u>: Frumento vescitur. Labore fruitur. Duobus amnis manebo. Hoc perficiet quinque diebus. Morte dignus est. Praemio dignus est. Parvi hoc erni. Centum denariis hoc emi. Centum denariis damnatur.